MW00977029

Juan N. Cortina
and
the Struggle for Justice in Texas

Carlos Larralde
and
Jose Rodolfo Jacobo

KENDALL/HUNT PUBLISHING COMPANY
4050 Westmark Drive   Dubuque, Iowa 52002

Photographs are from the J.T. Canales Collection. Used with permission of Carlos Larralde

Para

Jose Tomas Canales (J. T.)
1877-1976

attorney, historian, civil rights leader,
and a friend and inspiration
to the Hispanic community

Juan N. Cortina and the Struggle for Justice in Texas

Contents

Contents, Cont.

Acknowledgments

It is a pleasure to acknowledge the debts that have been incurred in the course of this research project, based largely on the work of the distinguished south Texas attorney Jose Tomas Canales. It was an honor to discuss the Cortinistas with Canales at great length. His unrelenting but insightful criticism made this project possible. As he used to say, : "There is no room for arrogance in the world of scholarship. There is no difference between a scholar and a student. To learn, one must be a student with the utmost humility and patience." Also, his valuable historical materials (that Carlos Larralde inherited) were essential. His private nurse, Delfina Treviño, must be credited for making these Canales visits extensive and for sorting out his historical notes, documents and photographs for discussion.

We must also single out several individuals in south Texas for special gratitude. Virginia Reyes Esparza, the granddaughter of Sabas Cavazos, Cortina's half brother, shared her family anecdotes. An archivist in Cameron County Courthouse, Ziola Tijerina, and Gilberto and his wife, a San Benito public school system administrator, Clara Zepeda supported and encouraged this project to help people understand that "setting the record straight" is both an exacting task and a labor of love. In addition, we acknowledge David Mycue, Curator of Archives & Collections, Hidalgo County Historical Museum for his valuable assistance.

As experts on 19th Century Mexican American history, Paul Vanderwood and Richard Griswold del Castillo's support is greatly appreciated. We especially thank Griswold del Castillo for his extraordinary patience as we discussed the subject year after year. His editorial skills, encouragement and continuous analysis improved this manuscript and made this project more meaningful. We thank James Evans for sharing his research on Juan Cortina as written in pulp novels. Finally we thank Jerry L. Madison for his aid.

Jose Rodolfo especially wishes to thank his new bride, Melanie Jacobo, for her love and support. Also, gratitude is extended to David Vega who helped in the project.

We extend our sincere gratitude to those individuals who inspired and believed in us: Mike Ornelas, Tom Davies and Richard Griswold Del Castillo. Of course, we do not forget our loved ones. We acknowledge these individuals for helping us preserve some of Jose Canales historical research on Juan Cortina (other Canales data on Cortina is now part of Charles Goldfinch's thesis on Cortina). Any inaccuracies in telling this remarkable story are our own, not a reflection of the distinguished assistance we received along the way. All of these individuals have helped to rescue Cortina's life story from oblivion to help make it become a recognized part of the American experience. In the end, we hope we revealed Cortina's passion for justice for all people and especially along the United States-Mexico border.

Introduction

Some years ago, one of the authors of this book, Carlos Larralde was urged by his grandparents to dig into his family's history. Together with his family they leafed through a photo album of family and friends recalling the rich heritage of their past as well as the region in which they resided, the lower Rio Grande Valley. Carlos' attention quickly focused on his renowned cousin, one Jose Tomas Canales, a Brownsville attorney who had enjoyed a high profile in state politics since the turn of the century. With a degree in law from the University of Michigan, Class of '99, Canales practiced law in Cameron County's seat at Brownsville. People elected him their representative to the state legislature for several terms, 1905 to 1912 and then 1917 to 1920. It was in the last term that Canales made his most memorable mark, thundering against the atrocities committed by the formerly untouchable Texas Rangers, who had rampaged the Valley during the so-called "bandit raids" of 1915 and 1916, depriving the citizenry--almost all Hispanics--of their dignity and human rights in the name of Ranger justice. Canales described the wanton depredations, one of the sorriest chapters in the region's history, a history that has never been fully told for fear of retribution. But J.T. Canales raised enough of a ruckus at the time to get the legislature to disband the old style Rangers and then have them reconstituted along other lines, which, in many ways, became only slightly less controversial than their former ones.

Throughout his long life, Canales remained an ardent crusader for Hispanic rights in the Valley. He sponsored state legislation to halt real estate frauds by land companies that were largely supported by big money from outside the Valley as they tried to monopolize the region's agricultural potential. He sponsored other laws aimed at corrupt country and district judges throughout south Texas. Folks appreciated his endeavors so much that they called Canales "judge," a huge symbol of respect for the man and an indication of whom *they* wanted to be *their* judge.

As a legal defender of his own heritage, Canales had to know the history of his people, and so with him professional necessity became an avid avocation. Then, because it is not hard to fall in love with the history of the Lower Rio Grande, his passion led him to write and publish books on aspects of local history; Bits of Texas in the Melting Pot, parts one and two (1950 and 1957 respectively) and Character Builders, and Leaders of Men (both 1959). But nothing about the region interested him more than the life of one of the Valley's most celebrated characters, the indefatigable Juan Nepomuceno Cortina, a man who dominated affairs in Mexico's neighboring state of Tamaulipas during the third quarter of the mid-nineteenth century sending thunderous reverberations into the valley on the U.S. side of the line. Cortina just happened to be one of Judge Canales' relatives.

Canales soon learned that those who had already written on Cortina had not treated the man kindly; they had pictured him as a greedy, political opportunist who had misused his authority and ignored the common person. However, the more he studied Cortina, the more Canales found that his predecessor had been misrepresented, so Canales aimed to set the record straight in a little book he published in 1951, Juan N. Cortina--Bandit or Patriot? Canales' answer to that question was very much to see Cortina as a patriot. It was not just a matter of finding the good which is in every human, but Canales found Cortina to be remarkably even-handed, and benevolent toward those he governed, even if he was also a tough, pragmatic politician when circumstances demanded it. Moreover, he felt that Cortina showed a special sensitivity toward Hispanics and their culture, especially those who were threatened by Anglos who were building a power base in South Texas. In sum, Canales liked the man, which is not to say he exactly modeled himself after Cortina, but who's to say one way or the other.

Because surveyors struck oil on a piece of his property, Canales had the wherewithal to buy up what documentation he could find on the life of his favorite historical figure, Juan Cortina. And over time he acquired an admirable and valuable library. The problem was that Canales was getting on in years--still plenty vigorous to be sure, but now moving deeper into his 80s. It's about this time that young Carlos Larralde knocked on his cousin's door in search of family history. For the next few years on weekly or monthly visits, Carlos listened raptly (and took notes) as Canales expounded on Cortina. Together they poured over the documentation in the attorney's personal historical holdings. But this was no father-son relationship; it was friendly enough but not warmly sentimental. It was more mentor and student, meaning disciplined, hard, no-nonsense work. Canales even dressed the part of the tough tutor--reserved and formal, all of which left Carlos bewildered, beleaguered, awed, but most of all, determined to get it right, to tell the story of Juan Cortina through the engaging and fertile mind of his cousin. The result is this book.

When in 1976, Canales died at the wondrous age of 99, he willed his splendid Cortina collection of papers and books to Carlos Larralde and charged his protege with setting the record straight on one of the valley's most illustrious historical figures. It took Carlos some time to do it. He left the valley for a formal education in California and finished with a Ph.D. in sociology from University of California, Los Angeles (UCLA). As at the time, college teaching positions were hard to come by, Carlos shifted to real estate, but still taught part-time at schools like Long Beach State University, all the while he continued his pursuit of Juan Cortina. Building on the holdings passed to him by J.T. Canales and mining the information from acclaimed archives such as the Bancroft Collection at the University of California, Berkeley. Carlos, worked to re-write the book manuscript with Jose Rodolfo Jacobo, a Chicana and Chicano Studies Instructor at San Diego State University. Together they laboriously pieced together the puzzle that is Juan Cortina. A good many of the pieces are still missing, some of them quite large and central to the Cortina story. But here we have a start, and we can begin to see the outlines of this truly remarkable human being.

Juan N. Cortina

Throughout this work one can sense J. T. Canales in the background, driving his young cousin to the task. So what we have here--and this is its special worth to the history of the lower Rio Grande Valley--is an interpretation of Cortina by one of his astute admirers reinforced by the documented discoveries of a present-day scholar, Carlos Larralde. The result is a marvelous story, nicely told, and for all of us, an original and significant contribution to our knowledge of a region that is certainly among the most unique and fascinating anywhere. Here we have a book which encourages us to experience and celebrate the grand diversity of the lower Rio Grande, both in its historical past and mesmerizing present.

Paul J. Vanderwood
Professor of History
San Diego State University

Chapter I

"Cheno"

The era following the United States-Mexican War (1846-1848) was characterized by an ever growing yet changing kaleidoscope of violence and injustice against the Mexican population. This socio-economic and political environment was the product of Manifest Destiny and its explicit premise of Anglo political, racial and moral superiority, a premise which had led directly to the military confrontation. Throughout the Southwest there occurred gross violations of basic human rights as well as rights guaranteed by international treaty. The Mexican government, concerned about the future of the Mexicans who would remain in the ceded territories after the war, and about the protection of their rights and property, had secured Articles VIII, IX, and X in the Treaty of Guadalupe Hidalgo. These articles dealt specifically with the civil and property rights of Mexicans now under American rule. The treaty, designed to end the calamities of war and establish the guarantees of the former Mexican citizens was, however, largely ignored. Indeed, violations of the Treaty of Guadalupe Hidalgo took place in every corner of the former Mexican territory.

For example, in California, the Gold Rush attracted a wave of immigrants, many of whom were from Sonora, Mexico, a region with a rich mining tradition. Economic competition and the sentiments associated with Manifest Destiny immediately led to an anti-Mexican, nativist attitude among the Anglo population. Moreover, little was done to distinguish among the newcomers and legal residents and citizens of Mexican descent. In the absence of a well structured and impartial legal institution, *Mexicanos* suffered the repercussions. Repression came in the form of direct violence at the hands of the citizenry or in the form of institutional litigation such as the Foreign

3

Miners' Act of 1850. Clashes occurred over the rights of the former Mexican citizens, many of whom had become United States citizens by rights established under the Treaty of Guadalupe Hidalgo, as well as over the validity of their land grants.

Throughout the former Mexican territories, land disputes were at the center of almost all clashes, and ill feelings emerged between Americans and Mexicans because the property rights of *Mexicanos* were ignored by United States government authorities and laypersons alike. A complicated and totally alien legal system (English Precedent Law vs. Hispanic Code Law) often led to costly cases in which the Mexican land owners lost the very land they were trying to retain. In short, the decades following the United States-Mexican War, were ones in which the Mexican community experienced displacement and injustice in the new social order. Not surprisingly there was resistance to such conditions. There were numerous groups and individuals who confronted the American occupation of their soil. One of the most renowned and successful resistors to the new American socio-political structure was Juan Nepomuceno Cortina.

Cortina was born on May 16, 1824, in the border town of Camargo on the Mexican side of the Rio Grande. This spacious terrain is on the western edges of an alluvial delta. This coastal plain embraces some of the richest soil in the world, including immense cotton fields. Here, Juan Cortina's family owned livestock and over a thousand acres of land. His father, Trinidad, a shrewd, hard working attorney, died when Cortina was a young man. Young Cortina was raised by his mother Estefana Cavazos, a strong and fearless woman who possessed a keen interest and great acumen in business and politics. In time, Juan Cortina would become an aristocratic rancher and family man in this region of violent hurricanes, bitter winter "northers", and suffocating humid summers.

Throughout his life, Cortina exhibited leadership values which were more instinctive rather than the product of any formal training. Noted scholar, Walter Prescott Webb, wrote that Cortina's qualities combined with a flair for leadership, "the disposition of a gambler, an eye for the main chance, and a keen intuitive insight into the character of the Mexicans, made him a man of destiny." [1] Cortina's upbringing and experience nourished his authority and persisted to provide his greatest strength. It was his love for the land and his charisma, however, which eventually gave him unparalleled fame and notoriety in the region both among his compatriots and his enemies.

Numerous documents attest to Cortina's charisma and leadership skills. Benjamin F. McIntyre, a soldier in the Union Army, wrote of Cortina in 1864, "In appearance he is of medium size, about 40 years of age... he is a genial companion but a man of a few word... he is a daring intrepid soldier and inspires those under him with confidence." [2] The Brownsville *Herald* echoed popular sentiment when it noted that Cortina "was a man of very few words, and the silence he maintained on any and all occasions led to the belief that he was a man of deep knowledge. There is no doubt but that he possessed a large amount of common sense, and he was also a good judge of men." [3]

Throughout his early life, then, Juan N. Cortina stood as a complex individual with an endless drive and energetic mind. Jose Tomas Canales stated it well when he wrote that Cortina, "disciplined himself to become a model of a good soldier, which enabled him to weather the hardships of military life. It made him a hardened man and a heroic figure to his people. He could be methodical, persistent, and clearheaded under intense pressure. Cortina had a skill that could almost remove himself from reality as if he was staring at himself." [4]

Not everyone, however, believed that Cortina was worthy of such glowing accolades. For many he was a thief and a merciless assassin. Texas Ranger N.A. Jennings wrote in 1899 that "About three thousand robbers were under him and he was virtually the ruler of the Mexican border." [5] An article in the Corpus Christi *Ranchero* stated that under Cortina, the area had been sacked for hundreds of miles and its inhabitants ruthlessly murdered." [6] But the answer to the enigma of Cortina's life lies in the study of the United States-Mexican War and in particular the post war period. The end of the United States - Mexican War did not bring an end to the ideologies and hostility which in part led to the conflict. Instead, the end of the war brought on a variety of new attacks on the Mexican community and gave rise to bitter resentment. In a climate of violence, flagrant prejudice and unrestrained abuses against Mexicans, the emergence of organized resistance was inevitable. The situation all along the Rio Grande was extremely volatile. The only real obstacle to the emergence of a movement of resistance and retribution was the rise of a charismatic leader. In fact, such resistance was already solidifying around a man named Juan N. Cortina whom the people in the lower Rio Grande called "Cheno."[7] This man, according to historian Jerry Thompson, became the leader to the poor *vaqueros, campesinos*, and the general illiterate persons of Mexican descent on both sides of the lower Rio Grande, who had nothing but poverty, exploitation, and suppression.[8]

Cortina believed fervently that he had a responsibility and a need to dedicate his life to the welfare of Mexicans whose lives were being destroyed by the post-war occupation, and much of the Mexican community in the region gave their support to Cortina as defender of Mexican rights, one who would free them from American control, amend grievances, and punish the enemy. The Texas Ranger John Ford said clearly that "to the poor who heard him, Cortina was a sign of hope in a land where hope heretofore had no meaning." [9] Ford further recounts:

> *Sometimes Cortina would make a speech in the market place and the poor would listen intently to what he had to say. He would not harm the innocent, but would fight for the emancipation of the hungry peons along the border. . . After Cortina and his body guard rode away, the peons seething with hatred for the Americans, returned to their baked fields and mud huts to await his signal for them to follow.*[10]

Congressional records from 1859-1860 document that Cortina was seen as a remarkable leader in south Texas as early as 1848. An 1860 affidavit states that "a certain movement . . . in 1848 tended to impress the Mexicans on this [Texas] side of the river with the idea that Texas had no [legal] claims" to the territory. Juan Cortina was cited as one of the leaders of this movement advocating separate territory and full rights for Mexicans. Obviously, the idea, and its leader, worried American government officials because the affidavit describes Cortina as a man to be "feared . . . on account of his political influence." [11] It would appear that authorities were well aware of the probability of resistance and violence against the new social order and that their fear of a charismatic leader fomenting a revolt was clearly justifiable

On both sides of the Rio Grande (but especially in the north), Cortina became and remained a feared and disreputable rebel, a reputation fueled by racism, propaganda, and journalistic excess. All helped to promote an ever worsening picture of Cortina, as can be seen in early 1860, when Robert E. Lee, while trying to maintain peace in Texas, alluded to the conflicting ideas of "that myth, Cortina."[12] During the American Civil War, a California historian, Nicholas Herdeman, wrote, "a short ride from the Rio Grande brought them (Confederate soldiers) face to face with the greatest danger extant in that region. They suddenly found themselves surrounded by a fierce looking ring of bandits from the guerrilla gang of the notorious 'Red Robber of the Rio Grande,' Juan Cortina." [13]

A number of early contemporary references to "Cheno" depict him as a bandit. Writings of that period include such characterizations as: "the most daring as well as the most illusive Mexican bandit . . . that ever wet his horse in the muddy waters of the Rio Grande;" "a notorious guerrilla;" and, "the scourge of the lower Rio Grande valley." [14] Nevertheless, in an otherwise dismal portrait of Juan Cortina, writer Lyman W. Woodman did make this concession: "For all of his rascally and evil ways, Cortina did retain one commendable trait; he had a deep love for his country and wanted to see it prosper under a fair and peaceful Mexican administration." [15]

More recent works on Cortina reflect a much more favorable view of the man. In 1980, Arnoldo de Leon wrote that "Cortina's movement, then . . . called attention to a government that had deviated from the democratic principles it espoused. In this respect, the rebellion was similar to Shay's rebellion, the Whisky Rebellion, and the Texas Revolution." [16] Cortina was outraged upon observing the treatment Mexicans received at the hands of the Americans, realizing that he and his fellow countrymen were without civil rights under the new social order. Anglos controlled the police force and the courts and many considered the mistreatment or even the killing of Mexicans no crime.

Historian Pedro Castillo asserted: "Cortina led and organized a revolt and was a man fulfilling what he felt was his duty...both resisting the Anglo and standing up for the rights of his countrymen." [17] Cortina believed that under the American control of the region the *Tejanos* would not know peace, a fact recognized by the Corpus Christi *Ranchero* which reported in 1860 that Cortina had "sworn in his wrath, that since he cannot enhance the dominions of the serpent clutching eagle, by removing the boundaries of Mexico eastward, he will not allow Americans to enjoy any privileges in the valley of the Rio Grande. It is very easy for his guerrilla bands to carry his threats into execution." [18]

Still a majority of scholars have failed to recognize that Juan Cortina was only a symbol of political resistance. He personified the struggle against an injustice that was all too common. Cortina and his followers, as well as other groups and individuals, were in a struggle for justice, in a place were justice did not exist for most *Mexicanos*. Cortina simply took this struggle to a higher level. Indeed, his fame was such that he would be blamed or praised for the political deeds of Pedro Garcia, Apolinar Hernandez, Gregorio Villareal, Octavio Zapata, Adrian J. Vidal, and numerous others associated with Cortina who resisted and fought the oppression of the new social order. The most successful of these individuals was one of Cortina's followers on the Texas side, Carlos Esparza, who directed guerrilla warfare against the Texas Rangers. [19]

"Cheno"

The *Cortinista* movement, as the struggle for justice led by Cortina became known, survived numerous attempts to destroy it, including attacks, bribes, and false promises, by powerful economic and political interests. The opposition, notwithstanding, underrated the personal power of Cortina and the strength and devotion of his followers.[20] In the end however, incumbent Mexican President Porfirio Diaz, fearful of Cortina's power, ordered Cortina arrested and brought to central Mexico in 1877 where he could be watched. Cortina was later imprisoned for suspicion of revolutionary activities and died in 1894 at the age of 70. He was buried with military veneration in the Panteón de Dolores near Mexico City.

What follows is a detailed account of the man, Juan Nepomuceno Cortina. But more than that, it is a study of the motives that led this highly respected man to take up arms against the American forces. We begin with the United States-Mexican War.

1. Walter Prescott Webb, The Texas Rangers: A Century of Frontier Defense (Austin: University of Texas Press, 1965), 177

2. Nannie M. Tilley, ed. Federals on the Frontier: The Diary of Benjamin F. Mcintyre, 1862-1864. (Austin, Texas: University of Texas Press, 1963), 293.

3. Brownsville *Herald*, March 10, 1894. See also David A. Williams, David C. Broderick: A political Portrait (San Marino: Huntington Library, 1969), 7. Like Cortina, he was "a quiet man: and had some familiar qualities."

4. Jose Tomas (J. T.) Canales Interview (with Larralde), April 6, 1964. See also the San Antonio *Express*, October 25,1878.

5. N.A. Jennings, A Texas Ranger (New York: Charles Scribner and Sons, 1899), 139.

6. Corpus Christi *Ranchero*, January 14, 1860.

7. "Cheno" is a term of endearment.

8. Jerry Thomson, Vaqueros in Blue & Gray (Austin: Presidial Press, 1976), 13.

9. Stephen B. Oates, ed., John Salmon Ford, Rip Ford's Texas, (Austin: University of Texas Press, 1963), 309.

9

10. Ibid., 308-309.

11. Affidavit of W.W. Nelson, Brownsville, January 17, 1860, U.S. Congress, House Executive Document, 36th Cong., 1st Sess., No.52, "Difficulties on the Southwestern Frontier," Vol.7,1859-1860, Serial Number 1050 (Washington, D.C., Thomas H. Ford, Printer, 1860), 123.

12. This remark was made to his wife, Betsy, in Virginia. See Douglas Southall Freeman, R.E. Lee A Biography. (New York: Charles Scribner and Sons, 1936), 87. The remark is also quoted in Philip Van Doren Stem, Robert E. Lee: The Man and the Soldier, A Pictorial Biography (New York: Bonanza Books, 1963), 119. For most of Lee's letters relative to Juan Cortina see: John H. Jenkins, ed., Robert E. Lee on the Texas Border,1860 (Austin: Jenkins Publishing Company, 1988). Also, J. Lee Stambaugh and Lillian J. Stanbaugh, Lower Rio Grande Valley of Texas (San Antonio: NaylorCompany, 1954), 103-104. The Stambaughs also give an account of how writers have depicted Cortina. As an item of interest, see the biographical sketch of Cortina from 1859 to 1866 in the Matamoros *Ranchero*, May 18,1866,1.

13. Nicholas Perkins Hardeman, Wilderness Calling; The Hardeman Family in the American Westward Movement, 1759-1900 (Knoxville: University of Tennessee Press, 1977), 253.

14. Canales Jose, Juan N. Cortina: Two Interpretations(New York: Amo Press,1974),4. Reprint of Juan N. Cortina 1824-1892: A Re-appraisal, by C. W. Goldfinch, originally presented as authors thesis (M.A.), University of Chicago, 1950; of Juan N. Cortina presents his motion for a new trial, by J.T. Canales, first published in 1951 in San Antonio.

15. Quoted in ibid., 12.

16. Arnold De Leon, They Called Them Greasers: Anglo Attitudes toward Mexicans in Texas, 1821-1900 (Austin: University of Texas Press), 53. Shays Rebellion, which took place in Massachusetts in 1786 and 1787, was a revolt by debtor farmers against their creditors and especially against high taxes. Property owners and farmers faced imprisonment since they could not pay their debts.

17. Howard R. Lamar, ed., The Reader's Encyclopedia of the American West (New York: Thomas Y. Crowell Company, 1977), 264.

18. Corpus Christi *Ranchero*, May 26, 1860.

19. Canales Interview, April 10, 1964.

20. James R. Douglas, "Juan Cortina: El Caudillo de La Frontera." M.A. thesis, University of Texas, 1987, 109-110.

The life of Juan Nepomuceno Cortina can only be understood within the context of the events of his time - the Texas Rebellion in 1836 and the United States-Mexican War, 1846-1848. Having secured independence from Spain in 1821, the Mexican government viewed as vital the incorporation of the far northern territories. Mexican authorities believed that by increasing the population, the region would develop, thus securing it from foreign threats. Failing to attract its own citizens to the remote region, the government looked outward and passed a colonization act on August of 1824. The law offered land, exemption from taxes for four years, and security to foreign settlers. Ironically, the passage and success of this act all but guaranteed the loss of Mexico's northern territories to the United States. American immigrants failed to obey the conditions set by the Mexican government and, in turn, the Mexican government failed to consolidate its control over Texas. As early as 1826 a revolt took place in Texas by Anglo colonists who were critical of the Mexican government. While the Haden Edwards Revolt, as it is known, was short lived it was nevertheless a presage of things to come as the interests of the colonists and the Mexican government increasingly came into conflict.

Cultural collision and the beliefs associated with the doctrine of Manifest Destiny created an atmosphere of discord and violence that culminated with the declaration of Texas independence in 1836 and ultimately with a war between the United States and Mexico, the catalyst for which was the United States annexation of Texas in 1845. Mexican authorities had never recognized the independence of Texas

11

and the annexation by the United States was seen as an absorption of Mexican territory. Moreover, the disputes over the exact boundaries of Texas brought the Mexican and American military into direct confrontation. This clash gave rise to president Polk's cry that American blood had been shed on American soil which led to formal declaration of war against Mexico on May 11, 1846.

While a number of North Americans were opposed to the war on the grounds that it was immoral and unjust, the American Congress, echoing popular sentiment, overwhelmingly voted in favor of a declaration of war. The conflict led to Mexico losing one half of her territory, including the land Mexican authorities had planned to incorporate into the nation state through the passage of the 1824 colonization law. That territory now composes the states of California, Arizona, New Mexico, Texas, Nevada, and Utah as well as parts of Wyoming and Colorado. The conflict and its repercussions have shaped binational politics for the past 150 years and continue to be a cause for resentment even today.

During the war, the United States soldiers-mainly from Texas-brutalized the Mexican population. The number and variety of these sources which document this experience are extensive. In 1846, a correspondent for the Charleston *Mercury* wrote that United States soldiers in Matamoros were responsible for "murder, robbery, and rape . . . committed in the broad light of day."[1] Months later, the military correspondent of the New Orleans *Picayune* reported that Gen. Zachary Taylor's forces had "committed . . . outrages against the [Mexican] citizens of the most disgraceful, and character-stealing . . . insulting women, breaking into houses."[2] One account in January 8, 1847, stated that in Camargo "assassinations, riots, robberies, etc., are so frequent that they do not excite much attention. Nine-tenths of the Americans here think it is a meritorious act to kill or rob a Mexican."[3] The degree of violence even disturbed officers. In letters to Julia Dent, Lt. Ulysses S. Grant, described the great number of murders committed by volunteers and Texans. In one such letter Grant wrote, "I would not pretend to guess the number of murders that have been committed upon the persons of poor Mexicans . . . but the number would startle you."[4]

The primary problem facing the officers was the lack of discipline of the military volunteers. General Zachary Taylor, for example, had endless difficulties. In a letter to the War Department, on May 23, 1847, Taylor complained about the atrocities of the volunteers. "I have found it entirely impossible to enforce . . . the repeated orders . . . against marauding and other irregularities."[5] Later in a dispatch to the War Department on June 16, 1847, he remarked, "I deeply regret to report that many of the twelve month volunteers, in their route hence to the lower Rio Grande, have committed extensive depredations and outrages upon the peaceable inhabitants. There is scarcely a form of crime that has not been reported to me as committed by them."[6] George Gordon Meade, a Lieutenant under Taylor, complained that the volunteers were "always drunk . . . and killed for their own amusement." He was "disgusted with Taylor's poor discipline."[7]

The abuses persisted and the depredations did not stop at the Rio Grande. "Between Matamoros and Monterrey," according to one report, "nearly all the ranches and towns are destroyed."[8] . On May 11,1847, the Boston *Times* published a letter from General Taylor stating that, "under Col. Mitchell's command, the 1st Ohio along with some Texas Rangers, made prisoners of twenty-four Mexicans at Guellapea, gave them a mock trial by night, and then shot them through the head!"[9] From Monterrey, Irvin McDowell, a young army officer, wrote on February 27, 1848, that from Parras to the Rio Grande, "a band of American . . . deserters . . . were ravishing the women, and committing every species of atrocity on the defenseless inhabitants."[10]

In central Mexico too there were many atrocities and outrages committed by United States troops. General Antonio Lopez de Santa Anna in a letter to General Winfield Scott wrote: "I have with pain and indignation, received communications from the cities and towns occupied by the army of your excellency, upon the violations of temples consecrated to the worship of God; upon the robbery of the sacred vessels and profanation of the images, venerated by the Mexican people."[11]   In 1848, Santa Anna also complained that American troops had looted several cities and abused women in violation of the armistice. Finally he noted, "I have guarded silence until now, for the purpose of not chilling a negotiation that gave hopes of terminating a scandalous war, which your excellency has justly characterized as unnatural."[12]   News of atrocities echoed throughout Mexico. The invaders it seemed were embarking in a racial and religious war where few rules applied. "Anti-Catholic sentiment was a particularly chronic tenet of Americans' faith in themselves, and in Mexico many officers and men got their first look at a Catholic country."[13]

In central Mexico, General Winfield Scott "inflicted punishment upon several Americans for outrages upon the unoffending inhabitants of the country."[14]   Concerning treatment of the locals at the hands of the North Americans, journalist Loring Moody stated that "bitter experience has taught the poor Mexicans that it has been thus far no better than that afforded to sheep, by a pack of hungry wolves."[15] General Scott as well as other officers of the United States Army left damaging evidence of the brutalities committed against the Mexican population. Scott contended that his comrades had "committed atrocities to make Heaven weep and every American of Christian morals blush."[16] He claimed, "Murder, robbery, and the rapes of mothers and daughters in the presence of tied-up males of the families have been common all along the Rio Grande."[17]   Testimony by Lieutenant George C. Meade, later of Civil War fame, corroborated Scott's claims; Meade referred to the volunteers as "a set of Goths and vandals without discipline" who turned his regiment into "a terror to innocent people."[18].

Sadly, the fate of the people mirrored the fate of the Mexican military. Despite fierce fighting the Mexican forces suffered horrible losses and devastating defeats. Ulysses S. Grant admitted: "I had a horror of the Mexican War . . . only I had not moral courage enough to resign."[19] Grant wrote in 1847, "There is no force in Mexico that can resist this [American] army. The Mexicans . . . if they were well drilled, well fed and well paid, no doubt . . . would fight . . . they are put to the slaughter without avail."[20] He went on to state: " With an able general the Mexicans would make a good fight, for they are a courageous people."[21] The brutality of the war lasted until its conclusion in 1848 and in some areas well after, most particularly in the ceded territories where the carnage barely subsided with the conclusion of the war.

By many accounts the United States conquest of Mexico constituted no less than a brutal and indiscriminate attack upon the population. Scholar Jovita Gonzales wrote that the "Mexicans considered the Americans in Texas as intruders, vandals, [and] aggressors waiting for the opportunity to deprive them of their personal possessions, as they had denied the mother country a whole province."[22] These feelings added greatly to the postwar turmoil.

After the signing of the Treaty of Guadalupe Hidalgo in 1848, and the end of the declared war, Manuel Crecensio Rejon prophesied the future of the Mexican American:

Our race, our unfortunate people will have to wander in search of hospitality in a strange land, only to be ejected later. Descendants of the Indians that we are, the North Americans hate us, their spokesmen depreciate us, even if they recognize the justice of our cause, and they consider us unworthy to form with them one nation and one society, they clearly manifest that their future expansion begins with the territory that they take from us and pushing (sic) aside our citizens who inhabit the land.[23]

By most accounts, Rejon would prove to be correct.

The United States-Mexican War has been blotted out by a number of historians who apparently see it as part of a tragic event

Juan N. Cortina

during the era of Manifest Destiny. As Glenn W. Price explained, "Americans have found it rather more difficult than other people to deal rationally with their wars. We have thought of ourselves as unique, and of this society as specially planned and created to avoid the errors of all other nations."[24] Of the war, Carey McWilliams states "It should never be forgotten that, with the exception of the Indians, Mexicans are the only minority in the United States who were annexed by conquest; the only minority, Indians again excepted, whose rights were specifically safeguarded by treaty provision."[25]

In contrast to the United States, however, the war remains highly controversial in Mexico. Recently, in revised textbooks distributed by the government, a desire to placate the United States and encourage a free trade treaty agreement is evident. No longer is United States "imperialism blamed ... for the loss of Texas, California, Arizona and New Mexico."[26] The seizure of Mexico's land is blamed as much on Mexico's weakness and disorder as "on greedy imperialists to the north. These textbooks are part of a program to encourage a generation of school children to think of the United States as a friendly trading partner, "not an arrogant Goliath that swallowed up much of Mexico's richest land."[27]

The Legacy of a Treaty

On February 2, 1848, Mexico signed the Treaty of Guadalupe Hidalgo ending the United States-Mexican War. The agreement stipulated that the Rio Grande and Gila River were part of the new border between the two countries. By ratification, the United States acquired a territory two and a half times as large as France. The Mexican Cession included vast mineral resources in California, Nevada, New Mexico, and Colorado. Also zinc, copper, oil, and uranium were discovered in other parts of the Southwest. Parts of this area, including the central valley of California and the Mesilla Valley in southern New Mexico, contained rich farmland.

Articles VIII, IX and X of the treaty protected the rights of Mexicans who now found themselves in the American Southwest, and there was a particular emphasis on the protection of property rights. Judge Jeremiah S. Black stated, "The pledge was not only that the government itself would abstain from all disturbance of them but that every blow aimed at their rights, come from what quarter it might, should be caught upon the broad shield of our blessed government."[28] In reality, however, gross violations of the Treaty of Guadalupe Hidalgo took place and clashes over land were soon an all too common occurrence.

After 1848 violent episodes erupted between *Tejanos* and Anglo-Texans all along the Rio Grande. According to historian Richard Griswold del Castillo, "The Cortina Rebellion, in the Brownsville-Matamoros area in the 1850s and 1860s and the El Paso Salt War in the 1870s pitted entire communities against the Texas Rangers in a struggle for the land." Griswold del Castillo goes on to state that "hundreds of lesser struggles that resulted in lynchings, beatings, and riots also had their origin in conflicts over the land."[29]

Tejano families found their lands threatened since many had been forced to flee Texas during the Mexican War. For most, the decision to reoccupy their land in 1848 was an expensive one. It meant selling some of their lands to pay back taxes and dealing with a foreign and hostile judicial system. From these absentee owners and other relatives, American speculators floated high-interest loans, assumed mortgages on portions of the ranch, or purchased sections at tax sales. Most of the time this was done through fraud, confiscation, or simply by murdering the owners.

Prominent scholar David Montejano wrote, "In the immediate postwar period . . . the Rio Grande settlements attracted the worst elements among the Anglo pioneers."[30] A Brownsville priest, Abbe Emanuel Domenech, observed, "The Americans of the Texas frontiers are, for the most part, the very scum of society--bankrupts, escaped criminals, old volunteers, who, after the Treaty of Guadalupe

Hidalgo, came into a country protected by nothing that could be called a judicial authority, to seek adventure and illicit gains."[31]

The despotism of the Anglos and their intense brutal subjugation of the Mexicans persisted. This oppression was not only a rational excuse to seek grazing land for settlements and farming, but it also demonstrated an intense phobia and hatred for Mexicans and Indians alike. They were perceived as skilled at committing the most barbarous deeds. Gripped both by deep-seated fears and an intense desire for retribution, Anglos responded with horrible atrocities and used rebellions such as Cortina's as a pretext for more violence.

Extreme racism also played a major role in the post war conflict. Major William H. Emory stated in a <u>Report on the United States and Mexican Boundary Survey</u> in 1859: The "white race" was "exterminating or crushing out the inferior race." Others echoed his remarks. A United States soldier in the same year noted that "the Mexican, like the poor Indian, is doomed to retire before the more enterprising Anglo Americans."[32] Frederick Olmsted noted that Mexicans were seen "not as heretics or heathens to be converted . . . but rather as vermin, to be exterminated."[33] Mexicans were bitterly resented for their amalgamation or assimilation through miscegenation. Edward B. Foote wrote in his renowned, bulky medical reference book on the subject of marriage that the Mexican "population is divided between Mestizos, Mulattoes, and Zamboes, many of whom are but little above the savage, go naked, have no established forms of marriage . . . Those who do not associate with and imitate the customs of the whites, are omnigamic, and governed by their impulses."[34]

These statements were often supported by distinguished scholars such as Joseph Simms, who compiled a massive, celebrated college textbook that went through ten editions. Those of Indian background, Simms wrote, had a face that "clearly betray a degenerate nature."[35] He stressed that "Dark races, like the Indian and Negro, are naturally revengeful, like the elephant; and black eyes evince more or less a revengeful disposition."[36] He concluded that dark people especially those of Indian blood had "a wide mouth, in a narrow face, [that] may safely be defined as indicative of animal imitation."[37] Since Mexicans were viewed as inferior, they were merely excluded from the human race. Their physical appearance and conduct made it possible to regard them as repulsive. In 1874 for example Edward King and J. Wells Champney noted how the Mexican in San Antonio could not be made to see that "his slow, primitive ways, his filth and lack of comfort, are not better than the frugal decency and careful home management of the Germans and Americans who surround him."[38]

The violent treatment of Mexicans by Anglos in antebellum Texas was widespread. "Stories of Texas violence circulated throughout the United States, and even in England" adding to Texas' poor reputation.[39] In 1860, writer J.F.H. Claiborne asserted that "Civilized communities provide guardians for the helpless and imbecile, and defenses against the lunatic and the outlaw," and consequently it was the American duty to conquer and rule such a country as Mexico, "with or without her consent."[40] James Rawls wrote, "This sequence of events was hardly unique to the [Texas and] California frontier. Similar situations have existed elsewhere on Anglo-American frontiers and, for that matter, throughout human history. Fearing the savage without, if not within themselves, 'civilized' men have destroyed 'savages' with a special fury."[41]

Not surprisingly, with such views of the Mexican race, there was no law that truly protected the Mexican community. As early as 1850, Texas ignored the legal protections of the Treaty of Guadalupe Hidalgo. Seeing this, Governor P.H. Bell appointed a commission to investigate land claims in South Texas arising from the treaty. "The Bourland-Miller Commission, created by the legislature, gathered abstracts of titles and made recommendations to the Texas legislature. More than 135 claims were reviewed and presented to the legislature for confirmation."[42] Although most grants were confirmed, a number of claims rejected by the Texas legislature became issues of further litigation and later added fuel to what became the *Cortinista* struggle that would plunge most of south Texas into guerrilla war.

Juan N. Cortina

1. Loring Moody, Facts for the People. . . The Mexican War (Boston: Anti-Slavery Office 1847), 109-110.

2. Ibid.

3. William Jay, A Review of the Causes and Consequences of the Mexican War Boston: American Peace Society, 1850), 230.

4. Ulysses S. Grant to Julia Dent, July 25, 1846 in John Y. Simon, ed., The Papers of Ulysses S. Grant (Carbondale: Southern Illinois University Press, 1967), 1:102.

5. Abriel Abbot Livermore, War With Mexico: Reviewed (Boston: American Peace Society, 1850), 148.

6. Ibid., 234. In 1849, Charles T. Porter recalled that "the march of our army to the Rio Grande was a deliberate and intentional act of war against Mexico." See Porters work, Review of the Mexican War (Auburn, New York: Alden & Parsons, 1849), 79.

7. Nancy Scott Anderson and Dwight Anderson, The Generals: Ulysses S. Grant and Robert E. Lee (New York: Alfred A. Knoff, 1988), 77.

8. Ibid., p.232. Also, Martha A. Sandweiss, Rick Stewart, and Ben W. Huseman, Eyewitness to War: Prints and Daguerreotypes of the Mexican War, 1846-48 (Fort Worth, Texas: Amon Carter Museum, 1989), 103-120.

9. Moody, Facts for the People, 134.

10. Livermore, The War With Mexico, 151.

11. Ibid., 155.

12. Ibid.

13. Anderson and Anderson, The Generals, 83.

14. Ibid., 135.

15. Ibid., 134.

16. Carey McWilliams, North from Mexico (New York: Greenwood Press, 1968), 102.

17. Ibid.

17. Ibid.

18. Bernard Devoto, The Year of Decision: 1846 (Boston: Little, Brown and Company, 1943), 103.

19. Grady McWhiney and Sue McWhiney, eds., To Mexico with Taylor and Scott. 1845-1847 (Waltham, Massachusetts: Praisdell Publishing Co., 1969), 3.

20. Grant to addressee unknown, (August 22,1847) in Papers to Ulysses S. Grant, 144.

21. John Russell Young, Around the World with General Grant (New York: The American News Company, 1879), 2:162.

22. Jovita Gonzalez, "Historical Background of the Lower Rio Grande Valley," *LULAC News* (September, 1932). In 1866, George Lunt wrote, "To be sure, by the treaty of Guadalupe Hidalgo, ratified at the termination of the war with Mexico, the Rio Grande was afterwards agreed upon as the future boundary between that country and the United States, ... Mr. Tyler, however, had seen fit to adopt that river as the boundary, without taking the trouble to seek any adjustment of preliminaries with Mexico." George Lunt, The Origin of the Late War: Traced from the Beginning of the Constitution to the Revolt of the Southern States (New York: D. Appleton and Co., 1866), 141-142.

23. Antonio de La Peña y Reyes, Algunos Documentos Sobre el Tratado de Guadalupe Hidalgo (Mexico: Sec. de Rel. Ext., 1930), 159, quoted in Feliciano Rivera, A Mexican American Source Book (Menlo Park, Calif: Educational Consulting Associates, 1970), 185.

24. Glenn W. Price, Origins of the War with Mexico: The Polk-Stockton Intrigue (Austin: University of Texas, 1967), 7.

25. Carey McWilliams, North From Mexico, 103.

26. See Gregory Katz, "Mexican Textbooks play down Revolution and play up U.S.," Long Beach *Press-Telegram* (Long Beach, California), September 10, 1992.

27. Ibid. In the past, Mexico's official history was written "by leftist historians with a negative view of the United States. Now that trend has been reversed." Adolfo Aguilar, an academic and writer, said that it is time for Mexico to drop the concept of an official history text once and for all. "Why don't we let historians write the story and let teachers and administrators choose?" he asked.

28. Chauncey F. Black, Essays and Speeches of Jeremiah S. Black (New York: D. Appleton and Co., 1885), 468. After the war Americans remained contemptuous of Mexico. To them it was a failed republic. They thought that Mexico, however, might

be politically regenerated under the Anglo-Saxon conquerors. "Assuming that the United States was essentially Anglo-Saxon and that the Indian, Hispanic, and mestizo people of Mexico were inferior, these Americans explained Mexico's decline or could be made fit only by emulating Americans, who had a special cultural genius for republican liberty."

The Mexican War haunted Yankee politics for years, especially during the American Civil War. It reminded the United States that it might become as pitiable a failure as Americans held Mexico to be. Now the Confederacy and the United States would be in perpetual war, burdening the continent with "jarring, warring, fragmentary states," and conducting themselves as "a race of chieftains, who will rival the political bandits of South America and Mexico."

Gen. William Sherman saw American politics as absurd and wanted the United States to avoid "the fate of Mexico, which is eternal war." To him the failure of Mexico was a fate which the United States could never be sure of escaping. See: Charles Royster, The Destructive War: William Tecumseh Sherman, Stonewall Jackson, and the Americans (New York: Alfred A Knopf, 1991), 125-126.

One Civil War figure, Confederate General Gideon Johnson Pillow, was Gen. John B. Floyd's second in-command and was haunted by his mistakes during the Mexican War. In 1846, Pillow earned a reputation for incompetence while defending the village of Camargo on the lower Rio Grande. "He mistakenly ordered his men to build their breastworks on the wrong side of their trench leaving them exposed to the enemy." See David Nevin, The Civil War: The Road to Shiloh, Early Battles in the West (Alexandria: Time-Life, 1983, 87.

29. Richard Griswold del Castillo, The Treaty of Guadalupe Hidalgo: A Legacy of Conflict (Norman: University of Oklahoma, 1990), 83.

30. David Montejano, Anglos and Mexicans in the Making of Texas,1836-1986 (Austin: University of Texas Press), 31.

31. Quoted in ibid., 32.

32. McWilliams, North From Mexico, 105. In California, the same thing happened to some Hispanics and the majority of Indians. The San Francisco *Alta California*, December 5, 1850, wrote that the Indians must fade away "like a dissipating mist before the morning sun from the presence of the Saxon." Then in the following year the *Alta* (March 17,1851), forecast "certain doom" for the Indians. "They must fade away before the Saxon race as the cloud in the West before the light and heat of a greater power." See: James J. Rawls, Indians of California: The Changing Image (Berkeley: University of California Press, 1984). See his chapter "Extermination," 171-201.

One could only speculate if Foote were alive today and saw American society and read Richard Rodriguez, "Perspective on the Americas: The Indian Doesn't Need Your Pity," *Los Angeles Times*, October 11, 1992, what the reaction would be. Rodriguez wrote that "The first Americans were not hapless victims; their descendants are refining and redefining the European legacy." Then he wrote that five hundred years after Christopher Columbus set foot in the Americas, "Indians are alive and growing in number from the tip of South America to the Arctic Circle. If you do not believe me, look at brown Mexico City."

Also, Carlos Fuentes, "The Birth of the Hispano-Indian Civilizations of the New World, Los Angeles *Times*, October 11, 1992, wrote, "For the Indian cultures of the Americas, if it did not prevail, it did not perish, either. Rather, it became a part of what one might term the counterconquest, that is, the Indian response, to the purely European presence in the Americas."

35. Joseph Simms, Physiognomy Illustrated or Nature's Revelations of Character (New York: Murray Hill Publishing Company, 1891), 320. Originally written in 1872, Simms used three hundred elaborate engravings to support his data.

36. Ibid., 301.

37. Ibid., 126.

38. Edward King and J. Wells Champney, Texas 1874, An Eyewitness Account of Conditions in Post-Reconstruction Texas, Robert S. Gray (Houston: Cordovan Press, 1974), 108-111. For a comparison of how California treated its Indians, see: Rawls, Indians of California, 198.

39. Dickson D. Bruce, Violence and Culture in the Antebellum South (Austin: University of Texas Press), 103. Also, Mark F. Nackman, "Anglo-American Migrants to the West: Men of Broken Fortunes? The case of Texas, 1821-46," Western Historical Quarterly, No.5, (1974), 441-55.

40. Ibid., 174.

41. Rawls, Indians in California, 180. Rawls California chapters, "The Varieties of Exploitation" and "Extermination," reveal a familiar pattern to most 19th century conflicts in the American Southwest, especially in the treatment of Indians and Mexicans in Texas.

Recently Eduardo Garrigues, Spain's consul general in Los Angeles, wrote: "And, while some place responsibility for the decline in population of the California Indians on the Spanish colonization and the mission system, anthropologist Robert F. Heizer has shown that the real tragedy for the Indians came between 1848 and 1870, after the Gold Rush." Although the Treaty of Guadalupe Hidalgo guaranteed Chicanos their old grants, according to research by Patricia Limerick, author of "The Legacy of Conquest," "80%

41. Rawls, Indians in California, 180. Rawls California chapters, "The Varieties of Exploitation" and "Extermination," reveal a familiar pattern to most 19th century conflicts in the American Southwest, especially in the treatment of Indians and Mexicans in Texas.

Recently Eduardo Garrigues, Spain's consul general in Los Angeles, wrote: "And, while some place responsibility for the decline in population of the California Indians on the Spanish colonization and the mission system, anthropologist Robert F. Heizer has show that the real tragedy for the Indians came between 1848 and 1870, after the Gold Rush." Although the Treaty of Guadalupe Hidalgo guaranteed Chicanos their old grants, according to research by Patricia Limerick, author of "The Legacy of Conquest," "80% of those lands eventually fell in to the hands of American lawyers and settlers. In 1850, the Foreign Miners' Tax drove the Hispanic out of their mines." See Garrigues, "The Pathology of Hero-Making," Los Angeles *Times*, October 12, 1992.

As for hero-making in Texas history, the life of David Crockett has been so muddled in fantasy that it is difficult to separate fact from fiction. One scholar who studied this subject was Richard Boyd Hauck. See:Hauck,Crockett:ABio-Bibliography (Westport: Greenwood Press, 1982). Some of the fantasy started with a purported journal kept by Crockett and published as Col. Crockett's Exploits and Adventures in Texas. The diary, it turns out, was written mostly by Richard Penn Smith, who plagiarized material from other books.

American historians rarely used sources from the Mexican point of view. Finally the long-ignored eyewitness accounts left by Santa Anna's soldiers came to light. One such source is the account of Jose Enrique de la Peña . De la Peña pointed out that "Crockett did not surrender willingly, but he did survive the massacre, and he was executed." It was not the glorious death in the Alamo generally associated with Crockett. De la Peña's diary was carefully translated by Carmen Perry and published in 1975. Dan Kilgore, a past president of the Texas State Historical Association, carefully examined and interpreted the translation. "Mr. Kilgore tells us that the Texas Press and other parties who did not want the legend of Davy Crockett sullied responded with vehement protest to the publication of Carmen Perry's translation and the subsequent dissemination of these facts. Such an uproar is ludicrous but understandable."

42. Montejano, Anglos and Mexicans in the Making of Texas, 85.

CHAPTER III

The Texas Rangers

and the 'Criminal Gentry'

Despite the many accounts of atrocities and massacres of Mexicans, the violence and injustice inflicted on the Mexican community was not confined to the war and to those directly involved in military matters. The legal system and those who controlled it were also responsible for uncounted atrocities, abuses and indignities committed against the Mexican community. In an era of open hostility, Mexicans were commonly subjected to undeserved verbal and physical abuse. They were regularly suspected and often actually accused of a variety of crimes with little evidence or respect for the truth. To "control" the locals, the state of Texas commissioned the Texas Rangers, an organization of law-enforcement officers on horseback. The Rangers shortly accumulated a well-earned reputation for violence against the Mexican community. The Rangers were particularly violent during the United States-Mexican War. Of the Rangers, Zachary Taylor wrote after their departure from Monterrey: "We may look to the restoration of quiet and order in Monterrey, for I regret to report that some shameful atrocities have been perpetuated by them since the capitulation of the town."[1]

According to Jose Canales, the Rangers "tortured and slaughtered innocent people, even children suffered their torments. At times they violently ejected them from their homes, raping women and girls." He further states, "The Rangers had a knack to seek out and murder any hostile witnesses or destroy any documents that revealed their evil deeds. For years, numerous county courthouse clerks refused to file complaints against the Rangers, "this, in spite of numerous Mexican testimonials to the murder of friends and families at the hands of the Rangers." [2] Canales knew their history well. As a state legislator in the early 1900s, he initiated legislative efforts to reform the Rangers. According to Canales, "The purpose of the Rangers was to defeat, disillusion, and subdue the majority of the simple and uneducated Mexicans to prevent further resistance and to keep them listless and completely demoralized."[3] Of one, Ranger Bigford, Canales said, "The man saw Mexicans and rats as one species. He had no remorse for human life, especially when it came to the Cortinistas."[4]

The Brownsville *Herald* reported that Ranger Bigford had been involved "in the killing of a couple of Mexicans in Live Oak County in [18]92 without proper justifications . . . and was tried and acquitted, it having appeared that the killing was done by the Rangers through a mistake."[5] Through these "mistakes," numerous innocent *Tejanos* lost their lives and their bodies were discovered later hanging on a tree or simply dumped by the roadside. Sometimes, Canales asserted "they were mutilated for sadistic pleasure by Bigford and his men." He goes on to state, "No jurors would find them guilty for fear of their lives or they simply could not care less about the fate of these tragic Tejanos."[6]

One renowned scholar who echoes Canales remarks is Americo Paredes. Paredes illustrates how the Rangers were used by the Anglo ranchers and merchants who controlled south Texas. Like Canales, Paredes' research was based on oral traditions and documents. "That the Rangers stirred up more trouble than they put down is an opinion that has been expressed by less partisan sources," Paredes said.[7]

Other scholars have also done work on this topic. Rodolfo Acuña writes of the Rangers: "Their commitment was to keep order for an Anglo oligarchy. Violence served the interests of Texas capitalists as a means of maintaining a closed social structure that excluded Mexicans from all but the lowest levels. They recruited gunslingers who burned with a hatred of Mexicans, shooting first and asking questions afterward."[8] Arnoldo De Leon comments: "The Rangers' persecution of Mexicans remains largely an undocumented story, partly because Ranger records are not easily accessible to researchers." He added, "But the portrayal by observers who saw them in their times and the tales that have come down through the years within the Tejano community go some way in verifying the reputation of *los rinches*."[9]

"The Criminal Gentry"

In 1857, Governor Elisha Marshall Pease admitted that "there was no justice for the Mexicans in Texas." His statement could not have been more true. Mexicans in Texas were, by and large, left unprotected by the law. A great deal of the injustice was directly related to the issues and struggle over land rights. According to an account by William Arthur Neale:

> *When the land bordering on the north side of the Rio Grande became Texas property, thousands of immigrants came pouring in from the states as well as people returning from California dazed with the gold craze. All began to settle and partition the lands amongst themselves; all claiming squatter's rights on what they called vacant lands. Naturally the heir of the land resented the encroachment of the Americans and bad blood began to boil between the squatters and the rightful owners of the land.*[10]

Thus, it quickly became clear that Texas law practically encouraged intimidation and fraud in the dispossession of the Mexicans. Scholar

27

David Montejano has observed: "Not only did the new American law fail to protect the Mexicans but it was also used as the major instrument of their dispossession."[11]

One who enjoyed the benefits of this extremely biased legal system was Richard King. What made King successful was his alliance with the Rangers and the federal army. In doing so, he enlarged his ranch to over 500,000 acres "with a commissary and store, stables, corrals, carriage and wagon sheds, blacksmith's shop, and houses for five hundred workers and their families."[12] The ranch expanded to over eight counties, an area slightly smaller than the state of Delaware. The Corpus Christi *World* reported in 1878: "He buys a little land, and his neighbors mysteriously vanish whilst his territory extends over entire counties."[13] King and others initiated cattle stealing on the Mexican frontier. King was said to have had "in his service a large band; he makes use of it for depredating upon other people's cattle, by seizing all of the unbranded calves, which are then branded with King's brand, notwithstanding the ownership of the calves is shown by their following cows bearing other people's brands."[14] King blamed his crimes on those who resisted him such as Juan Cortina and his followers as well as on numerous innocent Mexicans who were hanged for crimes they did not commit. Most people who attempted to use the law to correct King's abuses themselves suffered the consequences.

The Mexican Border Commission reported that in 1873 "the laws of Texas offer no energetic remedies for this evil, and are insufficient . . . the laws of Texas against robbery have failed to produce effect, because the officials of the administration protect the seizures and robberies." [15] As president of the Stock Raisers Association of Western Texas, which established a private militia made up in part of Rangers called the "minute companies" to fight the so-called Mexican menace or bandits, King exercised tremendous influence over south Texas.[16] After they were disbanded, one Leander McNelly, a Ranger, continued to lead the men in violence against the Mexican community. These Rangers were known as *los rinches de la Kinena* (the King

Ranch Rangers).[17] Jose Canales maintained that King's Rangers enforced the law to their own whim, creating further atrocities. He personally knew eight innocent men who were hanged one time or another because the Rangers suspected them of a crime.

La Revista Universal of Mexico City was aware of the activities of the King Rangers, and reported their "hunger and thirst for justice for the frequent crimes of cattle stealing committed on the frontier, attributed maliciously to Mexicans." The newspaper also reported that King's vigilante bands burned *Tejano* ranches and murdered families without "any formula other than that accustomed by the Apaches."[18] On April 22, 1875, in the Nueces County area, Ranger N.A. Jennings, reported the "murdering of peaceful Mexican farmers and stockmen who had lived all their lives in Texas. These murderers called themselves vigilance committees and pretended that they were acting in the cause of law and order."[19]

Juan Cortina and his followers known as the *Cortinistas*, fought against these ranching barons and the atrocities committed by them. The *Cortinistas* and Indians responded with a fierce vengeance against their tormentors. J. L. Allhands wrote, "Many times the Kings had to flee to the block house which was located in the center of their property, and defended by a battery of artillery." He adds, "King, who traveled around with armed outriders as guards, was ambushed on many occasions."[20]

King and others like John McAllen, who owned 800,000 acres in Hidalgo County were often the target of the *Cortinistas*.[21] McAllen and other land barons lost over 100,000 head of cattle to the *Cortinistas* who used the animals to feed themselves and those who were in poverty. They also sold some of the livestock to purchase weapons. For Juan Cortina, the fight against these land barons was also personal. In 1848, Charles Stillman established the Brownsville Trading Company. In partnership with Simon and Jacob Mussina, the business acquired land, attracted investors, and drove up prices. In 1852, Stillman managed to take over a valuable portion of Brownsville itself, via the acquisition of acreage from the Espiritu

Santo grant, owned in part by Maria Josefa Cavazos and her husband, Rafael, relatives of Juan Cortina's mother.

Stillman never purchased the true deed to the portion of Brownsville. Instead he obtained squatters' claims, known as "labor titles" which were later declared void and worthless by the state as well as the federal courts. Afterwards when Stillman's lawyers, the firm of Basses and Hord, advised him that the Cavazos' title was the valid one, he refused to purchase it. Stillman compelled his lawyers to obtain the title for a consideration of $33,000 when the appraised value of the city property in 1850 was $214,000. Even then, the lawyers failed to pay cash. Instead they issued a worthless note.[22] Simon Mussina, Stillman's own partner, charged that it was a fake transaction and no funds were ever paid for the land. One thing is certain, the Cavazos owners never received any cash at all. Neither did they receive any part of the funds later paid by the United States government for the land in Fort Brown, which was supposed to have amounted to $160,000. Canales revealed that the money "through skullduggery or shenanigans of Charles Stillman was received by him and kept by him. With this wealth, thus acquired, Stillman made his famous fortune."[23]

Stillman was never satisfied. He renewed his assault on the Espiritu Santo land by defrauding Juan Cortina's mother of her interest for one dollar. The Cavazos family ended up "giving over" the remaining portion of the grant on which the city of Brownsville stood. "Fighting Stillman and company might have cost the owners of the Espiritu Santo Grant the entire grant, and the compromise was probably wisely consented to by them."[24] Cortina's family managed to retain some of their holdings, and the more conservative members were content to have the matter settled with the United States Supreme Court. Cortina, however, suspected that his family had been defrauded, and according to Canales, his suspicions were correct: "For there are indications that it was a series of clever legal maneuvers that gained Charles Stillman the land and that (Cortina's family) had to sacrifice to obtain even a measure of justice."[25]

Stillman proceeded to prosper in land dealings and, reputedly, in the traffic of stolen horses, for which Brownsville was a center. The Mexican Border Commission reported "In the years immediately following 1848, there were houses established in Brownsville for the traffic in stolen animals . . . that were to be carried into the interior of Texas".[26] One of Cortina's own relatives played a role in this story, Adolphus Glaevecke, a neighboring ranchman who had married into the Cortina family. Glaevecke, who was to become Cameron County Tax Assessor and Collector, as well as a member of the Brownsville City Council, "was heartily disliked by Cortina" as an opportunist and opponent of Mexican rights.[27] Glaevecke was an agent for buyers in the Texas interior, and employed thieves to steal horses in Mexico to meet the demand. "How vast this operation was may be imagined from the fact that Glaevecke had a large farm at Palo Alto in which dwelt ten servants who had charge of the animals until they were driven into the state."[28] The horses were transported for the most part across the "ford Tia Morales" near Brownsville. Glaevecke's operation is believed to have begun in 1848 and continued through the 1870s.[29]

An associate of Glaevecke, Thaddeus M. Rhodes (known to the *Tejanos* as *Teodoro)* became the first county clerk of Hidalgo County in 1852.[30] Rhodes hated Cortina and his followers, and, according to Canales, believed "every Cortinista should be shot on sight."[31] Rhodes gave shelter and protection to a group of robbers who "pillaged the farms of Reynosa and the villages of Nuevo Leon." "This band became at last so numerous and terrifying that in extracts taken by the Mexican Border Commission mention is made of depredations committed by them which clearly prove their audacity."[32]

According to the Mexican Border Commission, the military commander of Matamoros told the Mexican consul in Brownsville to urge the American government to devise a plan for "suppressing the robbers who collected on the frontier of the United States, dishonored the nation, and kept the Mexican authorities in a constant threatening attitude."[33] In response to repeated complaints, Judge J. F. George investigated horse stealing charges against Rhodes and "stolen horses were found in the enclosure belonging to Rhodes; the robbers resisted the Judge, who was compelled to use force, wounding two of their number in the fray. This placed Judge George in great danger."[34] Rhodes was jailed briefly as an accomplice "in the depredations committed by the band," but was soon freed and continued his illegal activities and his campaigns against the *Cortinistas.* Canales asserted that, "Rhodes encouraged the Texas Rangers to patrol the border against Cortina's men and to crush any further support to Cortina's cause."[35] As for Rhodes, the Mexican Border Commission report states:

> *Rhodes is now justice of the peace in the county of Hidalgo, and it appears that he had before acted in that capacity; he has also been collector of customs in Edinburg--notwithstanding his character has never varied. He has been notorious since the year 1840 for his illegal traffic in stolen animals, and for keeping in his employ men who made a business of robbing in Mexico, and his fame, in spite of his position, stays by him to this day. There are cases on file proving that the theft of animals is one of his objects in life, despite his social position.*[36]

It seems clear that as Jose Canales contended, "Mexican rights were trodden under the criminal gentry heels of power."[37] Some of these elite were Hispanics. An example was the elegant Mexican Francisco Yturria, an associate of Charles Stillman and owner of the powerful Yturria Bank in Brownsville which dated from 1853.[38] As a merchant, he had numerous assets in Brownsville and Matamoros and his remarks were sometimes the law. Like King and other Anglo gentry, Yturria was also involved in cattle rustling.

Another Hispanic businessman was Simon Celaya. W.H. Chatfield said that in 1865 Celaya's assets amounted to $1,200,000 and that he was later involved in the building of a railroad from Brownsville to Point Isabel.[39] The proper Spanish gentleman,

Celaya never understood why the local Mexicans were so rebellious. He clearly viewed the *Cortinistas* as absurd. Perhaps Canales summarized it best when he wrote that Celaya and Francisco Yturria "endeavor to satisfy their greed and were a major obstacle to bringing justice to the common man. They compensated the Texas Rangers to keep peace along the lower Rio Grande at whatever cost it took." [40]

These Hispanics were affluent and highly respectable personages. In a way, they were part of the princes of local trade and finance. They dressed elegantly and some, like Celaya, wore a monocle. They were disciplined, composed, hostile to change and jealous of their business privileges. At times, they expressed agitation at the *Cortinistas*, while smoking Cuban cigars and drinking from crystal goblets, filled with sherry or port. To them the *Cortinistas* were mute, sluggish, indifferent, rigid, and hostile to their business interests. In short, they too were enemies of Cortina's cause.

During the James Buchanan administration (1857-1861), these businessmen were encouraged in their deals at the expense of Mexican American rights. Buchanan "became increasingly enthusiastic for large slices of Mexican territory . . . (especially) Baja California, Sonora, and . . . a portion of Chihuahua." [41] Powerful and deep prejudices surfaced. The federal government remained indifferent to the civil rights of Hispanics and ignored completely the *Cortinistas'* cries for justice. *Tejanos* were clearly seen as an obstruction to Anglo progress. As Buchanan said, "It is beyond question the destiny of our race to spread themselves over the continent of North America, and this at no distant day should events be permitted to take their natural course." [42] Every step of the way, however, Buchanan's Manifest Destiny would be resisted.

1. Quoted in Robert Selph Henry, The Story of the Mexican War,(New York: Fredrick Ungar Publishing Co.,1950), 174. See also Moody, Facts for the People, 134. For more on the subject see letter of Zachary Taylor to Dr. Robert C. Wood, Matamoros, July 7,1846; letter of Zachary Taylor to Dr. Robert C.Wood, near Monterrey, Mexico, November 2, 1847, in the Zachary Taylor Correspondence, Huntington Library, San Marino, Calif. Most of these letters, primarily those cited here, were published in

Juan N. Cortina

William H. Samson, ed., Letters of Zachary Taylor from the Battle-Fields of the Mexican War (Rochester: The Genesee Press, 1908), 24, 149

2. Canales Interview, June 12, 1964.

3. Ibid.

4. Ibid.

5. Brownsville *Herald*, September 23, 1895.

6. Canales Interview, June 12,1964.

7. Americo Paredes, With a Pistol in His Hand (Austin: University of Texas Press, 1958), 31.

8. Rodolfo Acuña, Occupied America: A History of Chicanos (New York: Harper Collins, Publishers, 1988), Third Edition, 42.

9. De Leon, They Called Them Greasers, 76.

10. Reports of the Committee of Investigation Sent in 1873 by the Mexican Government to the Frontier of Texas (New York: Baker & Godwin Printers, 1875) 130-131.

11. John C. Rayburn and Virginia Kemp Rayburn, eds., Century of Conflict 1821-1913: Incidents in the Lives of William Neale and William A. Neale Early Settlers in South Texas (Waco: Texian Press, 1966), 64.

12. Montejano, Anglos and Mexicans in the Making of Texas, 52.

13. Montejano, Anglos and Mexicans in the Making of Texas, 79; Richard Harding Davis, The West from a Car Window (New York: Harper & Brothers, 1903), 131-32; J.L. Allhands, Gringo Builders (Iowa City: Privately Published, 1931), 21.

14. Corpus Christi *World*, May 23, 1878.

15. Reports of the Mexican Border Commission, 175.

16. Ibid., 105.

17. Acuña Occupied America, 30-31.

18. Ibid.

19. As reported in the Brownsville *Ranchero*, November 30, 1869. Also, San Antonio *Express*, February 2, 1875.

20. Jennings, A Texas Ranger, 130.

21. J.L. Allhands, Gringo Builders (Dallas, Texas: privately printed,1931) 20.

22. Ibid., 128.

23. Goldfinch, 36.

24. Canales, Juan N. Cortina Presents His Motion For A New Trial, 9.

25. Goldfinch, 37.

26. Ibid. Also, Stillman, Charles Stillman, 14-25. At first, the Espiritu Santo Grant went to the Texas Supreme Court. See the Brownsville *Ranchero*, February 22, 24 and 26,1870. See also the issues of March 1 and April 21, 26, 28 and May 5,1870.

27. Canales Interview, June 12,1964; Quotation is from Reports of Mexican Border Commission, 26.

28. J. Lee and Lillian J. Stambaugh, The Lower Rio Grande Valley of Texas,(Austin, Texas: The Jenkins Publishing Co.,1974) 104.

29. Reports of Mexican Border Commission, 28.

30. Ibid.

31. Ibid., 29.

32. Canales Interview, April 10,1964.

33. Reports of Mexican Border Commission, 29.

34. Ibid., 30.

35. Ibid., 31.

36. Canales Interview, April 15,1964.

37. Reports of Mexican Border Commission, 32.

38. Canales Interview, April 15,1964.

35

Juan N. Cortina

39. Stambaugh, Lower Rio Grande Valley. 92.

40. See also, Canales Interview, April 15, 1964. W.H. Chatfield, The Twin Cities of the Border and the County of the Lower Rio Valley (New Orleans: E.P. Brandao, 1893; reprint, Brownsville: Harbert Davenport Memorial Fund, 1959), 12. Only three original copies of the 1893 edition are known to exist. One was located by accident by Chauncey Stillman in an antique book shop in New Orleans in the early I 950s. He send it to the Brownsville Historical Association. Seeing the value of its contents, the association reprinted the book some 63 years after its initial publication. The reprinting was taken from copies of the original 1893 plates.

41. Canales Interview, April 12,1964.

42. Donathon C. Olliff, Reforma and the United States: A Search for Alternatives to Annexation, 1854-1861 (Alabama: University of Alabama, 1981), 85, 87.

43. Quoted in ibid., 86.

CHAPTER IV

Politics: Charisma and Religion

Community and individual reactions to the violence Mexicans endured during the late 19th Century were clearly evident throughout the Southwest. In Texas, Juan Cortina headed the struggle for justice and liberty. Aided by his charisma and the needs of the Mexican people, he became a symbol of liberation for the oppressed. Cortina established a political organization about 1848. According to Jose Canales it was known by the popular name *La Raza Unida*. It was also called *La Unificacion de la Raza* or *La Santa Raza Unida*, although it may have had other names when it was formed in what is now Cameron County.[1] It stood for unity, devotion to the community, mutual aid and brotherly love. Affidavits taken from descendants in the 1970s attest to the fact that the organization had a strong following among many influential families along the Lower Rio Grande. [2]

La Raza Unida was a term employed to strengthen a sense of ethnic consciousness and pride. In a social environment where Anglos saw Texas Mexican Americans as a separate race, Tejanos "were forced to redefine their loyalties on racial terms," much like Mexicans would do in Southern California. "La Raza connoted racial, spiritual, and blood ties with the Latin American people, particularly with Mexico," wrote historian Richard Griswold del Castillo.[3] In Texas, as later in California, *La Raza* implied membership in a cultural tradition that was separate from the *Anglo-Sajones* or *norte-Americanos*.[4]

37

Juan N. Cortina

According to Jose Canales, under Cortina the concept was carried further, from an emerging ethnic consciousness to a militant, civil rights oriented political force. "Cheno" Cortina saw *La Raza Unida* as a political group organized along an extended family pattern, with himself as the head or patriarch. "It was basically a nationalistic, aggressive, secret organization to promote political and economic power for the Mexican community."[5] Canales also believed that the organization originally developed from the militant *Defensores de la Patria*.[6] The *Defensores* were composed mostly of men and women who in one way or another had defended their country as soldiers, nurses or spies during the Mexican War.[7] The *Defensores* lasted from 1844 to 1851. By 1851, Canales argued that the group was now called *La Raza Unida* by several members.

Cortina believed that a clandestine operation, based on organization, discipline, and to some extent, fear, was necessary for the survival of the movement. On November 23, 1859, Cortina remarked: "An organized society in the state of Texas will untiringly devote itself, [to] its philanthropical purpose of bettering the condition of the unfortunate Mexicans."[8] One United States government document of the time stated that Cortina "professes to be at the head of a secret society, organized for this object . . . so these people (Cortinistas) have defied justice on either side of the river, and now, banded together in an imposing army . . . with experienced reactionary officers to direct his military operations."[9]

According to Jose Canales, *La Raza Unida* was an underground association and there was little doubt "that much of the Mexican population in Texas were united in a secret society, whose purpose was to expel the Americans from the Rio Grande, and that for this object they were in secret combination with some of the contending parties in Mexico, from whom they received arms and ammunition for their ulterior designs, the immediate discovery of which was not possible."[10]

The concept of *La Raza Unida* and the man Juan Cortina were inseparable; it was Cortina who gave structure, meaning, and direction to the organization. His appeal for a wider audience was successful. His message was universally understood by *Mexicanos*; if they united under a strong leader, with clear goals, the battle would be fought and won. To Cortina, a revolutionary guerrilla, the battle had to be just that--a battle, and not a metaphor. He believed that justice, civil rights, and economic power for the Mexican people could only be achieved through insurrection.[11]

Some of Cortina's followers, *Cortinistas*, were men who had lost their land to the *Norte-Americanos*. In retaliation, they attempted to confiscate property from the Anglos and also from some of the Hispanic elite whom they felt were equally guilty, if only by complicity with the oppressors. One observer stated that some landed Mexican families "learned to get along with the Americans by overlooking whatever misfortunes fell on the lower class of Mexicans."[12] Scholar David Montejano stated: "Retaining their property and benefiting from the American presence, the established families had little cause for complaint. Their loyalties were subjected to a difficult test with Cortina's rebellion in 1859. Some lent the war quiet approval while others organized the repressions of the uprising."[13] Even Cortina's family was split on this issue and he turned his back on many of them. His relatives became acquiescent members of the new Texan society, including his brother Jose Maria, who became Tax Assessor and Collector of Cameron County in 1858.[14]

The majority of *Mexicanos* in the lower valley, however, supported Cortina. They were called *peons, pelados,* or *greaser pelados* by the newspapers.[15] One newspaper contended, "They formed the class known as *pelados,* or *ladrones,* who can be governed only by an iron rod--by force or fear--as much to be dreaded by every American, as they are and always have been by every good Mexican."[16]

By 1856, *La Raza Unida* conducted its propaganda through the Rojos, a political party active in the lower Rio Grande, especially in the Matamoros area.[17]. They also organized and armed the people to

39

defend their interests. Violence was now becoming the norm of the day. Although there is no corroborating evidence, W.H. Chatfield wrote that, "the first border raid [in Texas] was organized by Cortina in 1857, but was repelled by the state troops promptly sent to the Rio Grande by Governor Houston."[18]

Apparently, the Cortinistas now posed a serious threat to the business schemes of men such as William Stillman and his associates who continued in their exploitation of the Mexicans on both sides of the border. In 1859, the Corpus Christi *Ranchero,* which represented upper class sentiment, reported that Cortina's "rebellion must be crushed out and disposed of forever and Cortina and each and all of his adherent outlaws . . . tracked, caught and exterminated, and this by the most prompt, energetic and efficient measures. The past has demonstrated the invulnerability of those outlaws . . . Fifty of these desperados . . . can successfully defend themselves, and can easily defeat a much superior force."[19]

Development of a *Cortinista* Ideology

Cortina as a leader served with courage and dedication. To his followers, he expressed their unspoken rage against all the oppressive forces which they endured. As they heard him articulate his beliefs they overcame their despair and regained faith and dignity. As a master orator, Cortina's speeches were impressive.[20] In September, 1859, Cortina in an eloquent speech, said in part, "Our hopes have been defrauded in the most cruel manner in which disappointment can make one effort [fight], and at one blow destroy the obstacles to our prosperity."[21] He concluded: "Innocent persons shall not suffer . . . Our lands, if they are to be sacrificed to the avaricious covetousness of our enemies, will be rather not so on account of our own vicissitudes . . . Our personal enemies shall not possess our lands until they have fattened it with their own gore."[22]

The emotion in Cortina's speeches resulted from his passionate dedication to his followers and their cause. Moreover, his dramatic flair was no handicap.[23] According to Canales, "Cortina's speeches aimed to inspire the Mexican people to fight. He spoke to incite political involvement and action at the immediate moment. He would improvise in order to react to his audience's questions. He often used parables with a political point, and sometimes jested to keep their attention."[24] John S. Ford comments in his memoirs about how Cortina authorized his appeals in both nature and religion. He writes, "He told them to love nature, for nature will always give us sufficient means to support our frames. They must love the land for the land was all they had. Yet the land-hungry imperialists to the north were out to take the land from them."[25] Also recorded in Ford's recollections are parts of Cortina's November 23, 1859 speech wherein he describes himself and his goals as part of God's plan:

"Mexicans! My part is taken; the voice of the revelation whispers to me that to me is entrusted the breaking of the chains of your slavery . . . the Lord will enable me, with a powerful arm, to fight against our enemies, in compliance with the requirements of that Sovereign Majesty, who, from this day forward, will hold us under his protection."[26]

Canales declared that "Cortina saw himself as a mystic with a mission in life to help his people. He believed that to save his soul, he had to aid his fellow countrymen. Even the Cortinistas saw him as a mystic."[27] Ford remarked that "in the beginning of his career Cortina was so successful that many of his countrymen were led to believe him to be the instrument in the hands of the Almighty destined to chastise the insolent North Americans."[28]

"To the Glory of God"

With his prayer book in hand, Juan Cortina presented himself as God's agent to his people. Cortina concluded that God spoke to him

Juan N. Cortina

through unforeseen visions. In reality, Cortina represented a despondent Mexican society who needed hope to survive and feel secure within themselves, while suffering from economic tribulations.[29] They were scorned by a distant Anglo government who saw them as an obstacle to progress. Major Samuel P. Heintzelman saw Cortina's followers "as thriftless and vicious and lived principally on jerked beef and corn, or beans for luxury." Others saw them as an listless, backward and as a fanatically religious people. Most of these destitute natives were considered felons without legal title or citizenship.[30]

In 1860, Francis Hardman wrote that Anglos in the region "saw themselves, with no very patient feeling, under the rule of a people both morally and physically inferior to themselves. They looked with contempt, and justly so, on the bigoted, idle, and ignorant Mexicans, while the difference of religion, and the interference of the priests, served to increase the dislike between the Spanish and Anglo-American races."[31] Religious differences were such that according to Historian Fredrick Pike, the New Englander, Daniel Webster even wondered if "wars, plagues and famines" which afflicted the Latin American population was not a punishment from God for their evil, savage, and immoral ways.[32] In some areas of Texas, to be a Catholic was the same as being a traitor. In reference to Mexico in 1861, the Corpus Christi *Ranchero* reported: "Not a wind blows over that God-forsaken, priest-ridden, anarchial country."[33]

Cortina realized the effectiveness of having politics and religion fused together. According to Jose Canales, a spiritualist-infused atmosphere flourished primarily on the Mexican side of the Rio Grande with numerous *curanderos* (spiritual healers). They carried banners with the image of the Virgin of Guadalupe, preaching the love of God or "to the glory of God," and our *"nuestra santa raza"* (our blessed race). The cross and the cult of the *Virgen de Guadalupe* manifested a powerful impulse that gave meaning to a rootless and oppressed Hispanic class. The *Virgen de Guadalupe* prevailed as the most successful unifying symbol for Cortina as the spiritual movements spread into Texas where turmoil prevailed.

42

Politics: Charisma and Religion

Juan Cortina knew when to make promises and use smooth words to get his people to accept the political situation. He had a great feel for the dramatic and was able to use this to his advantage. As Jose Canales noted, "Religion was his opportunity and it was the vehicle that gave him domination over his people. To them, these spiritual movements were their strength, their moral fiber to resist." [34] Cortina was too much a diplomat to forget his political platform. He never let his sacred ideas color his judgment with wishful thinking. To him and to his people, religion was a major source of courage and strength. Regardless, spiritual healers told the people that Cortina had been sent to them by God to save them from further American oppression. This was essential in organizing his resistance movement. Spiritual leaders went as far as to encourage people to place flowers or light candles before the image of Cortina with the rest of the saints on family home altars. Through their theological belief and sacred shrines, they molded the *Cortinista* movement with their religious zeal to obtain justice. They persisted with the Guadalupan cult to inspire the *Cortinistas* to combat their enemies.

1. The concept of La Raza remained popular in Texas long after the Cortinista era. Another realization of La Raza developed after 1920. See Antonio Castellano's article dated September 16, 1921, "Por la Patria y Por la Raza," in Mexico 1821-1921: International Commercial Edition for Furthering Commercial Relation between United States and Mexico (San Antonio: Revista Mexico), September 27,1921. Copies are in the Albert Bacon Fall Collection, Huntington Library, San Marino, California. Senator Fall tried to cite this article and other literature as offensive to the United States and reason to meddle in Mexican politics.

    Along the Lower Rio Grande region under Alonso S. Perales and other Hispanic leaders during the 1920s, the concept of La Raza continued to evolve. See Brownsville *El Cronista del Valle*. For articles such as "Seccion Editorial," "La Unificación de la Raza," September 18, 1927; "La Unificación de los Mexico-Texanos," October 12, 1927; "El Dia de La Raza," October 12, 1927. Apparently there was a conflict with braceros and deportations. See the issues of May 25, 1928, January 25,1929, and May 3, 1929. *El Cronista del Valle*, issue of February 21,1930, "Brillante Defensa de La Raza Mexicana" reported on the activities of Alonso Perales. Later in 1970, another perception of La Raza developed in Crystal City, Texas under Jose Angel Gutierrez which became a political civil rights crusade and spread to other parts of the Southwest.

2. Affidavit of Francisca Reyes Esparza, December 21,1973, San Benito, Cameron County, Texas; affidavit of Gilberto Esparza Zepeda, December 21,1973, San Benito, Cameron County, Texas; affidavit of Herman Montemayor, December 27, 1973, Brownsville,

Juan N. Cortina

Cameron County, Texas; affidavit of Pedro Garcia, Jr., December 29, 1973, Harlingen, Cameron County, Texas. All items are in the author's files.

3. Richard Griswold del Castillo, The Los Angeles Barrio 1850-1890: A Social History (Berkeley, California: University of California Press, 1979), 133-134.

4. For La Raza in California, see Griswold del Castillo, 133-34. For La Raza in Texas, Canales Interview, June 12, 1964.

5. Canales Interview, June 12,1964.

6. Ibid.

7. Ibid.

8. Reports of Mexican Border Commission, 133

   As stated in the preface, "This book is a translation, ordered by the Mexican government, of the reports presented by the commission. . . to investigate the depredations committed on both sides of the Rio Grande." This is a translation from Informe de." Champ Clark, The Civil War: Decoding The Yanks: Jackson's Valley Campaign (Alexandria: Time-Life, 1984), 23.+4646.

9. Reports of Mexican Border Commission, 139.

10. Canales interview, June 12,1964.

11. Ibid.

12. Montejano, Anglos and Mexicans in the Making of Texas, 36.

13. Ibid.

14. Canales, Juan N. Cortina, 6; Goldfinch, Cortina, 39, 67. As to the data in the footnote on page 67, Canales said it was a dispute over politics.

15. "G" wrote on October 30, 1859, referring to Cortina's men in those terms. The letter was published in the CorpusChristi Ranchero, November 5, 12, 1859.

16. Corpus Christi Ranchero, November 19, 1859.

17. Canales Interview, June 12,1963.

18. Chatfield, The Twin Cities of the Border, 2. Chatfield may be referring to Cortina's 1859 raid on Brownsville. Houston did not become governor until December, 1859.

19. Corpus Christi Ranchero, November 19, 1859.

19. Corpus Christi *Ranchero*, November 19, 1859.

20. Scholars failed to realize that Juan Cortina and a majority of Mexicans along the Lower Rio Grande spoke an arachic Spanish. For example, they would say *bivir* for *vivir* (to live), *beyer* for *beber* (to drink), *yave* for *llave* (key), *diso* for *dijo* (said), *muestro* for *nuestro* (our), *mozotros* for *nosotros* (we), *muez* for *nuez* (nut), and so on.

These words were part of a regional Ladino, an antiquated Spanish. It has survived through words like *guerco* (devilish child) and *asina* for as (which means "that way"). Marcela Trujillo, a student of linguistics, has argued that it is a rich, variegated frontier language, which is the key to the unwritten history of the Southwest. Trujillo said, "We need to make a linguistic map of the Southwest. The importance of this would be to explain why lexical items are peculiar to particular regions, and not so much that they are different. Thus we could begin to decipher the unwritten history of the Chicanos of the Southwest." Denver *Post*, January 7, 1973.

21. Proclamation of Juan Nepomuceno Cortina, September 30, 1859, "Difficulties on Southwestern Frontier," 72.

22. Ibid.

23. Canales Interview, May 10,1963.

24. Ibid.

25. Ford, Rip Ford's Texas, xxvi-xxvii, 308-309. A relative of John Ford, Ford Green wrote in "Rip Ford & The Last Battle of the Civil War," *The Armadillo*, May 11, 1983, 7, that Ford had "little formal education" and passed himself off as a medical doctor. Ford was a distinguished member of the Know-Nothing Party, and a member of white supremacy groups such as the Knights of the Golden Circle and The Order of the Lone Star. As a Knight, Ford worked for the acquisition of Cuba and northwestern Mexico as additional slaveholding territory. He wrote, "Slavery is right. It is an institution founded by God. . . The Bible is the strong-hold of the slave owner." See the Austin Texas *State Times*, February 21, March 21, 28, April 4, 11, 1857.

The headquarters of the Knights of the Golden Circle was in San Antonio. Secret meetings were held in several parts of Texas. A mayor target was the German-Texans. "The German population is large, and distinguished for intelligence and industry, and their opposition to slave labor, and for which, by recent events, they have been severely punished." "The Texas Treason," A Paper Read Before the New York Historical Society, June 25, 1861, by Major J.T. Sprague, United States Army in Moore, The Rebellion Record, 1:100.

The Knights, "were to make the South safe for slavery and. . . conquer Mexico as a side order." Two filibusters regiments of profiteering soldiers of fortune "were

Juan N. Cortina

actually armed and organized, but before they reached Mexico, they were diverted to another, bigger war." The Knights and other groups persecuted German-Texans who refused to support the Confederacy. These Germans fled and some joined Cortina. Ford continued to be a Knight since he "was star-following, pragmatic, restless, and apparently without an ideology of any kind. . . He had prejudices but no philosophy. Above all, he instinctively went where the action was." T. R. Fehrenbach, Lone Star: A History of Texas and the Texans (New York: The Macmillan Company, 1968), 338-374. Canales is the source for German involvement with the Cortinistas.

26. Ford, Rip Ford's Texas, 309. Canales believes that Ford copied this quote from the Corpus Christi *Ranchero*, December 3, 1859. This article is a reprint of the "Proclamation of Juan Cortina to the Inhabitants of the State of Texas." It was published in the Brownsville *Flag*, November 26, 1859.

Canales said that the value of this proclamation illustrates how Cortina saw himself and what was the purpose of his mission and his society, which was the Raza Unida.

27. Canales Interview, May 10, 1963. Cortina said the same thing about himself. See the Corpus Christi *Ranchero* December 3, 1859.

28. Ford, Rip Ford's Texas 276.

29. Geronimo also had visions and represented his oppressed Indian people in his militant struggle against their oppressors during the same era. His "exploits riveted the nation," wrote David Roberts, "Geronimo," National Geographic, October, 1992, 50.

30. Quoted in De Leon, They Called Them Greasers, 55. See Letter of S. P. Heintzelman to Joaquin Arguilles, February 9, 1860, Letter of Heintzelman to John Withers, February 10, 1863, Samuel Peter Heintzelman Papers and Journals, Library of Congress, Washington.

31. Francis Hardman, Frontier Life, or Tales of the Southwestern Border (New York: C.M. Saxton, Barker & Co., 1860), 171.

32. Fredrick B. Pike, The United States and Latin America: Myths and Stereotypes of Civilization and Nature (Austin: University of Texas Press, 1992), 75.

33. Corpus Christi *Ranchero*, March 9, 1861.

34. Canales Interview, April 12, 1964.

CHAPTER V

Cortinista Followers and Supporters

Cortina's struggle was more than just a reactionary act. It was part of a larger movement seeking justice for those *Mexicanos* in the lower strata of the socio-economic lower order. To those who understood this, Juan Cortina was a liberator, not a thief or an assassin, rather, Juan "Cheno" Cortina represented a collective ideology that fought against injustice.

Although Cortina remained the symbolic authority of his militant group, there were several individuals who held and openly expressed a variety of political opinions. A list of several leaders illustrate how their diverse styles and concepts molded the *Cortinistas*. Detailed biographical portraits of these organizers who simply jotted their reflections down on paper are understandably rare, but several do stand out. One was the pragmatic and cautious Carlos Esparza, who became one of Cortina's advisers. Esparza defined, elaborated and adopted various ideological concepts. He even endorsed a belief in utopian socialism.[1] While no record exists of Esparza's association with specific radical groups, scholar Gaston Garcia Cantu has documented the existence of socialist and anarchist groups in Camargo and Tampico in the 1850s. Moreover, by the 1870s, such progressive publications as *El Socialista*, *La Emancipación*, *El Hijo del Trabajo*, and the *Manifesto del Partido Comunista* were available along the lower Rio Grande.[2]

Well known radicals such as Carmen Huerta and Francisco Gonzales lived in the area during this period and influenced Esparza, Cortina, and others in the *Cortinista* quest. Canales reports that "during this era some *Cortinistas*, such as Andres Leal and Juan Ramirez proposed an experimental economic system which included the concepts of cooperative work and common ownership of certain essential farms and businesses. Under this system, an individual could only own a certain amount of property and earn a certain amount of money each year."[3]

The *Cortinistas,* like other movements, sought support, encouragement, and funds from all possible sources. In their search they crossed paths with the socialists or anarchists, and found they shared similar concerns about poverty, land use, oppression, and social justice. Recent research by historian John M. Hart has shed additional light on the socialist and anarchist movement in Mexico. He discovered that in the 1870s *El Hijo del Trabajo* was popular due primarily to the writings of Jose Maria Gonzalez. Jose Canales was convinced that such "radical newspapers" had an impression on the *Cortinistas* such as Carlos Esparza, Andres Leal, Juan Ramirez, Narciso Martínez, Juan Cantu and others.[4]

Hart wrote that "despite his importance, Gonzalez' background remains largely unknown. Although the record of his public activities and the numerous newspaper editorials and articles he wrote during the second half of the 1870s have left behind a historical-ideological legacy and a limited amount of biographical information. He emerges as one of the most provocative and controversial figures of his time."[5] In seeing Carlos Esparza's profile, we may be viewing the shadow of Jose Gonzalez. Both had proposals for the betterment of society and the uplifting of the lower classes. Gonzalez expressed his anarchist ideology in clear terms:

> *The Social Revolution.*
> *What is the Object of that revolution?*
> *To abolish the proletariat.*
> *Then, cannot the government pass laws to bring about this goal?*
> *The government is unable to do anything.*
> *Why?*
> *Because it is the first enslaver.*[6]

Several men influenced Gonzalez. One of them was Santiago Villanueva, the founder of Mexican fraternal societies, and Jose Munuzuri, an editor of *El Hijo del Trabajo*. Through them, he "serves as an example of the Spanish anarchist impact upon the Mexicans."[7] One can only speculate here that these men's crusade for justice would lead them to sympathize with the *Cortinistas*, and no doubt some of their articles reflect that. Also there may have been anarchist organizers helping the *Cortinistas* in the battle front and in labor issues. As Jose Canales asserted, "Here is one of the gaps of Cortinista history that is missing,"[8] John Hart explained: "An underground [organization] of anarchist and anarchist-oriented labor organizers has been found to have operated in the factories and mines from Veracruz to Sonora in the prorevolutionary era."[9]

The *Cortinista* allegiance was phrased with idioms written on colorful, artistic flags. Slogans in Spanish such as "Land and Liberty," "God, Cortina and our Rights," "United we fight for our Dignity as Men," "March on to Defend our Race against Abuses," "Long Live our Struggle for decent Laws," and numerous others were common. None of these flags survived, but Canales noted that another *Tejano* movement in the area during 1915, the anarchist *Magonistas*, used these old emblems. They designed new banners based on *Cortinista* concepts.[10]

Gringo Support

The *Cortinista* ideology became much more flexible as numerous *Norte Americanos* aided the *Cortinista* cause to achieve justice. The truth is that Juan Cortina did not "have a burning hatred for the Texans" or the *gringos* as some writers have asserted.[11] He did abhor certain *gringos* who were violent and stole from the Mexicans, calling them *gringos apestosos* (stinking gringos), who were "criminals covered with frightful crimes." He clearly wanted justice to penalize those *Americanos*.[12]

Juan N. Cortina

Throughout his career, Cortina sympathized and aided immigrants who escaped oppression in Europe. In turn, they identified with Mexicans who supported Cortina to gain justice. Thus, many of the *gringos* that joined the *Cortinistas* were German Texans or simply Germans. According to Jose Canales, one such individual was John Kaltenbach. He was born in 1786, in Baden, Germany, and he died on December 7, 1849 in Brownsville. As a merchant, he empathized with the Mexican population along the river. Another advocate was John Alsbach. He was born in Werther, Prussia, in 1828, and he died on October 3, 1858, in Brownsville. A Jewish merchant, Alsbach assisted the *Cortinistas* with funds.[13]

What bonded other German-Texans to *Tejanos* as friends was their resentment of the Know-Nothings, a popular political party between 1853 and 1857, which claimed there was a Catholic conspiracy to subvert American institutions. Anti-Catholic and anti-foreign in principle, the Know-Nothing Party wanted to prevent immigrants from voting and to stem further immigration. One can see a distrust of the Know-Nothing Party in the German and Mexican newspapers, mainly in the San Antonio and Austin area in such publications as the *Neu Braunfelser Zeitung*, *El Bejareno*, and *El Ranchero*. Another was the *Galveston Zeitung*.[14] As Walter L. Buenger stated:

Up until Cortina's raid on Brownsville, relations between Germans and Mexicans had been cordial. They had fought the Know-Nothings together and Germans had generally tried to defend Mexican Texans' rights. Cortina's raid strained but did not sever these bonds. Editor Lindheimer, the spokesman for stability and conservatism among the Germans, was careful to distinguish between "hostile Mexicans" on the border and other Mexican Texans. He tried to wait until all the evidence was in before passing judgment on Cortina, and he suggested that events had been magnified out of proportion.[15]

50

While different incidents and concepts strained their relationship, the *Cortinistas* had cherished Germans as noble friends since the Mexican War.[16] They renewed that loyalty to each other as fellow unionists during the American Civil War. Like the *Cortinistas*, the Germans had "not been assimilated into the Southern culture and therefore felt little loyalty to the Confederacy."[17] When Confederate officers began conscripting young Germans into the army in the summer of 1862, problems developed.[18] Like other dissenters, several of these German-Texans were whipped, shot or hanged by vindictive Confederate officials or vigilantes. Some protesters were shot as they knelt on their coffins or forced to build the fortifications at Galveston before being exiled.[19] Most of these German-Texans "made their way to Matamoros where they were protected and sent on to New Orleans or New York." For that part the *Cortinistas* hid them in isolated places where they were joined by other deserters from the Confederate forces.[20]

German-Texans and other Germans as well as other Americans joined the *Cortinistas* and fought with them against the Confederates. Jose Canales noted "They became good soldiers and Cortina cherished them as some of his best troops during the French Intervention in Mexico."[21] In 1865, the Imperialist Lieutenant Ernest Pitner recorded that in Matamoros "There are very many of our German fellow-countrymen here…"[22] Some Germans, and English by background, even assimilated into the Mexican culture. Two of Cortina's fiercest and most dedicated soldiers were Josiah (Jose) Turner and his brother William (Willie) Turner.[23] Known to the Mexicans as *Los Tanas*, the Turners were English by nationality and were originally from Maryland. At the age of nineteen, it was Josiah's "fortune to come with General Taylor from Corpus Christi to Brownsville in 1846, and he had an intimate knowledge of the facts pertaining to the battles of Resaca de [la] Palma and Palo Alto."[24] The brothers settled at the Galveston Ranch near Santa Maria, about twenty- five miles from Brownsville. Josiah married Maria Petra Treviño and William married Antonia Treviño, sister of Petra. The

Treviño sisters owned land in that area and engaged in agriculture to a large extent.[25]

In time, the Turners were assimilated into the Mexican culture and Josiah in particular came to identify with the *Cortinista* cause. By 1870 he spoke English with a Spanish accent. Instead of eating bread with his meals, he ate tortillas. He detested most of his fellow Anglos who were convinced that every individual Mexican was violent and dishonest. Despite his tranquil appearance, he was a dauntless guerrilla fighter and was always seeking to obtain arms for his fellow *Cortinistas*. Fortunately for the Turners, their activities were shrouded in mystery so they managed to survive the turbulent, political currents along the lower Rio Grande. Years later, Josiah, appearing as the stoic grandfather, would say, "My fellow *gringos* have seen the *Mexicanos* here with abhorrence and have seen them again with more malice and again seen them with more hatred that breeds more violence."[26]

Another staunch *Cortinista* disciple, George Atkinson, came to the Rio Grande from England in 1836 as a seaman on the freighter Morgan. He jumped ship and later married Maria Hinojosa in Matamoros. Three children were born of the marriage, one of them, Antonio, married Elena Chapa in 1860. Antonio and his father George were active as spies, scouts, and raiders for Cortina while Elena spent most of her time making bullets and nursing the wounded. The two other children, Francisco and Delfina, later went to Matamoros to join Cortina's army. Both were seriously wounded on the battlefield in the *Cortinista* cause. [27]

Another Cortina sympathizer, John Leonard Haynes, was born in Liberty, Bedford County, Virginia, on July 3, 1821, but grew up in Mississippi where he edited a newspaper. During the Mexican War, he served as a lieutenant. After the war he settled at Rio Grande City, where, according to historian Jerry Thompson "he became one of the community's more prosperous merchants . . . although not a Cortina partisan, he vigorously rejected the bitter anti-Tejano feelings of the state legislature and the Anglo settlement in Brownsville." [28]

In 1860, Haynes wrote newspaper articles in which he defended Cortina as a man of justice and argued that the 1859-1860 Cortina War was not a racial struggle. Rather, Haynes believed that the 1859 Cortina revolt was caused by "a deliberate attempt being made by certain persons to defraud them out of their lands, which attempt is sustained by persons holding high official position in the federal court." Haynes went on to say that Cortina was "fighting a few speculators, associated by a multitude of lawyers, who are endeavoring to rob the Mexicans of their lands."[29] Haynes hoped that the state of Texas would appoint a board of commissioners to investigate Cortina's grievances and thereby avoid violence. As he exclaimed, "This is no local measure, but affects the whole state, for a large number of troops have been ordered out to quell this rebellion, and the people of the state have a right to know why they are called upon to be taxed from fifty to one hundred and fifty thousand dollars, enough almost to support the government in time of peace for a whole year."[30]

The Brownsville *American Flag* on January 12, 1860, jeered Haynes as misguided, reckless, and little more than an eager politician. Later it wrote a sarcastic poem about "Poor Haynes" who was adhering to "Greaser grievances . . . for the purpose of investigating the title of lands . . . when charges and complaints to that effect had never been made."[31] This sneering attitude emerged again when the periodical announced the candidacies of Cortina for president and Haynes for vice president, "subject to the decision of the Matamoros convention."[32] This mock advertisement in the newspaper became a topic of jokes and further ridicule of Haynes who sought a peaceful solution to the *Cortinista* grievances. Still, Haynes had popular support from numerous groups including Texas political figures Sam J. Steward, J.B. McClusky, and David Thalheimer.[33]

Another supporter of Haynes was Robert Taylor, one of the commissioners sent by Sam Houston to investigate the *Cortinistas*. Taylor was distressed by the fact that the law failed to protect Mexicans in Texas. He too was belittled by the newspapers as a misguided fool who could not communicate with the "greasers" since he could not speak Spanish. His qualities as a public servant were also questioned.[34] One newspaper went so far as to refer to Taylor as one of the "ministers plenipotentiary to the court of Cortinas," located somewhere in the "amiable chaparrals" of the Rio Grande.[35] Taylor became a friend of Haynes and tried to stop further injustices against Mexicans in Texas.

Taylor wrote a report to that effect but he blundered because the other commissioner, Angel Navarro, was the son of Jose Antonio Navarro of Texas revolutionary fame who had aided the Anglos against his own people.[36] In order to advance his political career, Navarro called Cortina a thief and a murderer. Pushing Taylor aside, Navarro rewrote the report, arguing that Cortina was supported by the Mexican authorities and that Texas was being invaded by a Mexican menace. For those who favored Governor Sam Houston's supposed plan for invading Mexico and establishing a protectorate the tone of the revised Navarro-Taylor report was greatly appreciated.[37] Thus, Cortina's push for civil rights for Mexicans was now being used as a justification to invade Mexico.[38] Furthermore, there was the question of slaves fleeing into Mexico and somehow encouraging others to seek freedom south of the Rio Grande as well. "It would be well for planters to watch a little closer," asserted the Corpus Christi *Ranchero*.[39] In the end, however, Haynes and his supporters were overwhelmed with the American Civil War that devastated a nation.

As explained in greater detail below, during the Civil War there were other Anglo-Americans who aided the *Cortinistas* for personal and political reasons.[40] Among these was "Senior White" who, in 1874, encouraged the Mexican government to publish the Mexican Commission report to clear Cortina's name and to establish instead that it was the Texas Rangers and men such as Richard King who were the real criminals. As a publisher, however, White had limited influences as he only printed a limited number of copies for government officials.[41]

A number of Jews in Matamoros also assisted Cortina. As one anti-semitic British officer (Arthur Fremantle) noted in 1863, "Matamoros is now infested with numbers of Jews, whose industry spoils the trade of the established merchants, to the great rage of the latter."[42] European, or Yankee Jewish merchants, who had been victims of prejudice themselves, such as Bloomberg & Raphael and Emile Kleiber, were generous in giving money and supplies to the *Cortinistas*. Cortina respected them for their business experience, cosmopolitan knowledge, and facility with numerous languages. He used them as emissaries to deal with major American, Mexican or foreign officials.[43] There were other foreign businessmen who helped the *Cortinistas*, about whom Fremantle stated: "All these foreign merchants complained bitterly of the persecutions and extortion they have to endure from the government, which are, doubtless, most annoying; but nevertheless they appeared to fatten on the Mexican soil."[44]

In conclusion, it appears that a number of eclectic ideologies drove the *Cortinistas* and that their struggle was open to all who supported it. It also appears that while some foreigners were simply out to make a profit from the turmoil in the region, most of these Cortina allies were indeed faithful and committed to the *Cortinista* cause.

1.   Carlos Larralde, "The Thoughts of Carlos Esparza" Critica: A Journal of Critical Essays, Vol. 1, No.1 (Spring, 1984), 98. The historian Arnoldo De León wrote to the author, on March 29,1989, "Concerning Esparza, the scholarly literature has not picked up on his contributions. . . he lacks credibility because no other evidence corroborates your discovery."
      Yet the majority of Hispanic literary figures along the Rio Grande have been forgotten. The scholar Americo Paredes, in his two books With his Pistol in his Hand (Austin: University of Texas, 1958), and A Texas-Mexican Cancionero: Folksongs of the Lower Borders (Urbana: University of Illinois Press, 1976), have preserved several epic ballads for posterity.
      The work of Manuel E. Guajardo Tamaulipas Historia y Literario (Antologia) (Matamoros: privately published, 1932) has preserved portions of literary work of Maria Portales, Luciano Mascorro and several others who were popular along the Rio Grande. Articles such as Minnie Gilbert "Bethlehem on the Rio Grande," Ford

Times, December, 1961, 31-34, illustrate the once popular Spanish folk plays that are almost neglected today.

Along the Upper Rio Grande in New Mexico during the 1970s, Anselmo F. Arellano discovered the work of José Manuel Arellano, Manuel Salazar, José Ines Garcia and numerous others. Arellano publishes samples of their work in Los Pobladores Nuevos Mexicanos y sus Poesia, 1889-1950 (Albuquerque:Pajarito Publications, 1976).

Several scholars have stressed the loss of numerous records along the Rio Grande. For example, Carlos E. Castañeda, "The Human Side of a Great Collection," Books Abroad (Spring, 1940), 116,121, points out how many Mexican documents were lost or destroyed. Rodolfo Rocha in "Rio Grande Valley Historical Collection," Collection Newsletter, April 1, 1983 explains: "There is relatively very little history written about the Valley . . . particularly over the past one hundred years. The serious gap is the result of the lack of records and other historical documents covering that period. We are certain that such records exist and believe they are locked away in family trunks or stored in attics. These materials must be rescued and preserved before they, and the priceless information they contain, are lost to posterity."

Scholars such as Maria Teresa Marreno, Nicholas Kanellos and Clara Lomas attempted to collect and catalogue Hispanic historical collections that are scattered throughout the country. The Rockefeller Foundation has aided Kanellos after he spoke out about "the pressing need to locate and make accessible three centuries of Hispanic literature."

Literary works have continued to surface. They include a 19th Century novel, "the first American book with a Chicano theme, and *El Mississippi*, believed to be the earliest Spanish-language newspaper in the United States," which was published briefly in New Orleans in 1808. The first historic Spanish novel in the United States, Jicontencal, published about 1828 in Philadelphia, has also been saved. For more on this enterprise see Robert Epstein, "The Hunt for 'Who We Are' Project Hopes to Define U.S. Latino Heritage Through Rediscovered Writings," Los Angeles *Times*, March 4, 1992.

A Hispanic author in need of a biography is Felipe Maximiliano Chacón. In 1977, the scholar Doris Meyer accidently discovered his work at the Museum of New Mexico library in Santa Fe. Popular in the 1920s as a poet and a short story writer, Chacón has largely been forgotten. In 1984 his work was again printed to encourage further interest in this aspect of Chicano literature. See Doris Meyer, "Felipe Maximiliano Chacón: A Forgotten Mexican-American Author," in Ricardo Romo and Raymund Paredes eds. New Directions in Chicano Scholarship (Santa Barbara: University of California, 1977, 111.

Such valued yet forgotten writers continue to be discovered. A state senator and a book collector, Bennett H. Stern, edited Andrew Garcia, Tough Trip Through Paradise 1878-1879 (Boston: Houghton MifflinCompany, 1967). He wrote: "In 1948 I found the manuscript from which this book was written. It was stored in dynamite boxes, packed solid in the heavy waxed paper that powder comes in several thousand pages of legal-sized paper, both handwritten and typed." The account proved to be the story of an "adventurous Spanish kid from the Rio Grande" who recorded his recollections of Montana history. Black history has the same problem. See Lee May, "Turning a New Page in History," Los Angeles *Times*, May 14,1990. The author writes, "Prejudice and hardship buried the works of early black authors for years. But now, researchers are rediscovering the books and the truths they told."

2.   Gastón Garcia Cantu, El Socialismo en Mexico: Siglo XIX (Mexico: Ediciónes Era, 1969), 93, 338-39.

3.   Canales Interview, June 9, 1964.

4.   Canales Interview, June 12, 1964. Canales was intrigued with Carlos Esparza and compared him to the English writer William Shenstone, who wrote essays on men, manners and society.

5.   John Mason Hart, Anarchism & The Mexican Working Class, 1860-1931, (Austin: University of Texas Press, 1987), 63.

6.   Ibid., 63.

7.   Ibid., 64.

8.   Interview with Jose Canales, June 12, 1964.

9.   Ibid., vi. Recently a number of rare, Southwest Spanish-language newspapers were discovered at the Institution of Social History in Amsterdam. They had been placed there years ago by an Argentine anarchist who was researching the Mexican Revolution of 1910-1917. These papers could provide clues on the anarchist and socialist movement that may have influenced the *Cortinistas*. See Robert Epstein, "The Hunt for 'Who We Are,' Project Hopes to Define U.S. Latino Heritage Through Rediscovered Writings," Los Angeles*Times*, March 4, 1992. Most of Mexican history from 1845 to 1910 is still in need of additional research in relation to conflicts along the border with the United States. Other cultural aspects during this era have also been neglected. For example, the life of the most important Mexican painter of the 19th Century, Hermenegildo Bustos (1832-1907), remains a mystery. After his death he was largely forgotten until some research in the 1950s. "Almost nothing in English has been written about him, including many basic biographical facts. The most comprehensive study is a 1981 catalogue (in Spanish) by the eminent Mexican art historian, Raquel Tibol, for a show in Guanajuato, but it's long since out of print," said the Los Angeles *Times*, December 15, 1991.

10.   Brian Robertson, Rio Grande Heritage: A Pictorial History (Norfolk: Donning Company, 1985), 166. Robertson discovered this photo of a Magonista flag in the

Juan N. Cortina

12.   Ford, Rip Ford's Texas, 297, 309.

13.   Canales Interview, June 12, 1964. Canales learned of these individuals from elderly *Cortinistas* in 1898. As for dates, the author gathered this information along with Canales from the old Brownsville cemetery tombstones. Unfortunately the grave markers have recently suffered vandalism.

14.   Walter L. Buenger, Secession and the Union in Texas (Austin: University of Texas Press, 1984), 91.

15.   Ibid., 96-97.

16.   One German who distinguished himself during the Mexican War was Johann von Racknitz, known as Juan de Racknitz. He became a captain in the Mexican army. "His service record shows only that he took part on February 22 and 23,1847, in the battle at Angostura; in April in the battle of Cerro Gordo; and in August and September in the campaign for the capital of Mexico, rendering distinctive service on August 19 and 20 in the battle at Padierna. On December 2, 1848, at his own request, Racknitz was granted a discharge from the Mexican army." Later in 1851, Racknitz received a medal as one of the soldiers who "carried on the struggle against the North American invaders..." Before the war, Racknitz attempted to establish on the Nueces River a "Little Germany" with its own schools, its own hospital, churches, and even its own shipping company for commerce with Germany. Political events shattered his efforts. Also Racknitz used to travel to Matamoros and he probably had several Cortinista friends. See Louis E. Brister, "Johann von Racknitz: German Impresario and Soldier of Fortune in Texas and Mexico, 1832-1848," *Southwestern Historical Quarterly*, July, 1995, 77-79.

17.   Ford, Rip Ford's Texas, 338.

18.   R. H. Williams, With the Border Ruffians: Memories of the Far West 1852-1868, originally published (London:J. Murray, 1907), 232, 235, 239, 241.

19.   Richard B. McCaslin, Tainted Breeze: The Great Hanging at Gainesville, Texas 1862 (Baton Rouge:Louisiana State University Press, 1994), 128; San Antonio *Herald,* October 25, November 8, 15, 1862; August 10, 1863; *Clarksville Standard,* September 17, 1863; *Dallas Herald,* August 19, 1863; *HoustonTelegraph,* November 25, 1863. See also Frank Leslie's Illustrated Weekly Newspaper, February 20, 1864. All of these sources document the same oppression in other parts of Texas.

20.   Rupert Norval Richardson, Texas: The Lone Star State (Englewood Cliffs, 1956), 261. Canales, Interview, June 11, 1964; Canales Interview, June 12, 1964.

21.   Canales Interview, June 12, 1964.

Cortinista Followers and Supporters

22. Ernest Pitner, Maximilian's Lieutenant: A Personal History of Mexican Campaign, 1864-1867 (Albuquerque:University of New Mexico Press, 1993) 102. From evidence in what has survived of his writings, some of his letters and diaries were lost in Mexico. Also it is believed that Pitner wrote about his Mexican experiences after his return to Austria. No such material has surfaced.

23. During the early 1870s, enemies of the *Cortinistas* accused Jose Turner "with receiving horses stolen in Mexico." It was discovered that J. Siebert, city marshall in Brownsville, was charged "with complicity in the cattle robberies." As for Turner, "his good character for respectability is well established." See Reports of Mexican Border Commission, 6.

24. See "Birthday Of A Veteran: 84th Anniversary of Josiah Turner," Brownsville *Herald*, August 15,1910; Stambaugh, Lower Rio Grande Valley, 94. The newspaper account said that Turner "celebrated his birthday at his country home, the Galveston Ranch, about twenty miles from Brownsville. After a sumptuous dinner and supper there was an outdoor dance at night. In the center of the yard was placed the stalk of a maguey plant, thirty feet in height, with its beautiful top branches on which were suspended four large Japanese lanterns, rendering a most magnificent light for the entire yard. The effect was really fine."
    Canales, who had interviewed Turner several years earlier about his role as a Cortinista, attended the celebration. As the newspaper article said, "Mr. Turner's active mind is stored with a perfect mine of information upon those stirring days in Texas history, and his friends always enjoy a talk with him, when he is in reminiscent moods." Most of his recollections of the Mexican War were published in the Corpus Christi *Caller*, January 24, 1908. In 1910, Turner was the only survivor of Taylor's army living on the lower Rio Grande.

25. Canales Interview, June 12,1964. The Turner brothers were from Maryland. Married to the Treviño sisters, the brothers quickly assimilated into the Mexican culture. The marriage helped the sisters protect their property since the Turner brothers were familiar with the law and business practices of the region. Canales gathered his information from Maria Petra Turner, the daughter of Josiah Turner and Maria Petra Treviño. Born on the Galveston Ranch, Cameron County, on December 4, 1854, Maria Petra took an interest in Canales' historical projects. She died about 1920. For her birth record see the Immaculate Concepcion Church, Brownsville, Texas, Book 1, 168, no.243.

    The Brownsville *Herald*, August 15, 1910, has a biography of Josiah Turner. He was born on August 10, 1826 in St. Marys, Maryland and joined General Taylor in 1845. "Mr. Turner landed at Corpus Christi in December 1846. After the Mexican War was over, he decided to cast his lot in South Texas, locating in the Lower Rio Grande Valley, where he has lived ever since. He is the only survivor of Taylor's army living on this frontier. Mr. Turner's active mind is stored with a perfect mine of information upon those stirring days in Texas history, and his friends always enjoy a talk with him, when he is in a reminiscent mood." Turner died about 1920.
    During the 1870s, Turner was accused of horse stealing in Mexico. Justice of the Peace in the Third District, T. H. Hines said. "As regards to Jose Turner, his good

59

Juan N. Cortina

The Brownsville *Herald*, August 15, 1910, has a biography of Josiah Turner. He was born on August 10, 1826 in St. Marys, Maryland and joined General Taylor in 1845. "Mr. Turner landed at Corpus Christi in December 1846. After the Mexican War was over, he decided to cast his lot in South Texas, locating in the Lower Rio Grande Valley, where he has lived ever since. He is the only survivor of Taylor's army living on this frontier. Mr. Turner's active mind is stored with a perfect mine of information upon those stirring days in Texas history, and his friends always enjoy a talk with him, when he is in a reminiscent mood." Turner died about 1920. During the 1870s, Turner was accused of horse stealing in Mexico. Justice of the Peace in the Third District, T. H. Hines said. "As regards to Jose Turner, his good character for respectability is well established." See: Reports of Mexican Border Commission, 6.
In 1915, his wife testified in court on behalf of her relatives, Daniel and Bentruo Longoria, who were accused of aiding the militant Magonistas. "Mrs. Turner said that during the night of the fight and during the fighting both the defendants were in the room occupied by her and then when the firing commenced she instructed them to lie down on the floor and that no time during the shooting did either of them leave the room." Later she said that after the battle, "Daniel left the house and took whiskey, coffee, cots and pillows to the wounded soldiers." Brownsville *Herald*, October 11, 1915; *San Benito Light*, October 11, 1915.
On June 19, 1991, the author met the descendants of Josiah Turner. In 1993 Juan Longoria was still living at Santa Maria. Other members of the family had moved to Harlingen. See: Chatfield, Twin Cities of the Border, 41.

26.   Ibid. The last years of Josiah Turner were turbulent. His Galveston Ranch, not far from Brownsville, was the site for militant *Magonistas* who skirmished with the United States army during the blistering summer of 1915. Turner, however, was "in Brownsville on the day of the fight," Brownsville *Herald*, September 24, 1915. Although "a man of high standing," Turner and his family managed to survive the conflict while aiding the Magonistas. Still he remained forceful, with his mane of brittle white hair and his blustery optimistic nature, his bumbling witticism and his endless charity. In the end, his house was looted by the suspicious Texas Rangers to find evidence against the Turners. The Rangers dragged the furniture out on the front porch and cut up the upholstery, allegedly looking for concealed weapons. For more on the Magonistas, see: James A. Sandos, Rebellion in the Borderlands: Anarchism and the Plan of San Diego, 1904-1923 (Norman: University of Oklahoma Press, 1992).
The militant *Magonistas*, the *Sediciosos* considered Matamoros a sacred city since it was the center of *Cortinista* activities. Even when General Emiliano Nafarrate, commander of the Carranza forces, had to defend the city, he stated that he would fight for the city to the last man. He explained that no enemy would "acquire a single inch of territory in this city, the cradle of Servando Canales, Juan N. Cortina, and Manuel Gonzalez, and which has been crowned so many times with the unfading laurels of many triumphant glories." Brownsville *Herald*, March 23,1915.

The *Sediciosos* enjoyed listening to his speech. The *Cortinistas* were proclaimed the precursors of the Magonista movement. Old *Cortinista* veterans were honored with Mexican flag ribbons and invited as honored guests to a banquet. Flowers and candles were set before a portrait of Cortina. A few people gave speeches of those "glorious days." But these quixotic impressions disappeared on March 26-27, 1915, when a cavalry force of Villistas, numbering about 1000 men attacked Matamoros. Nafarrate won a fierce battle. Interviews with Martin Vela and Pilar Torres, September 12, 1964, San Benito. Both had attended the ceremony. For the turmoil in Matamoros, see: Brownsville *Herald*, March 26-28, 1915.

27.   Later, Antonio and Elena bought a tract of land east of Rio Hondo, which became the La Leona Ranch. Of the sixteen children who were born to the couple, several were named after popular *Cortinistas*. Of the sixteen children, most of them married and remained in the Rio Hondo area. Their descendants still live in the area and are proud of their *Cortinista* heritage.

The family data is from the family archives of one of the descendants, Doris Scott, Rio Hondo, Texas. Her relatives are related in one way or another to Aniceto Pizaña, a militant civil rights leader during the early 1900s. He influenced diplomatic relations between Mexico and the United States.

Other pioneer citizens of San Benito, Texas, Ismael Montalvo, Gonzala Noyola and Mateo Reyna were involved in cultural and political activities in the community. They shared their recollections of the Atkinsons who lived near San Benito.

28.   Jerry D. Thompson, Mexican Texans in the Union Army (El Paso: University of Texas, 1986), 13.

29.   Haynes, "Minority Report," in John Haynes Papers. The University of Texas, Austin, was able to save them, except for most of his correspondence. Haynes as a publisher, soldier, legislator and as an attorney remained loyal to the *Cortinista* cause.

30.   Ibid.

31.   Brownsville *American Flag*, January 12, February 9, 1860.

32.   Brownsville *American Flag*, March 17, 1860; Also, Haynes Papers.

33.   Galveston *News*, February 23, 1860; Also, Haynes Papers.

34.   The Intelligencer, n.d.,in "Haynes Scrapbook." See also the Corpus Christi *Ranchero*, February 25,1860.

35.   These quotes are from undated newspaper articles in "Haynes Scrapbook."

36. It was rumored that Governor Houston wanted Jose Antonio Navarro as the commissioner "to round out the victory won by the Texas Rangers over Mexican bandits." Instead his son Angel was dispatched. "The battle between the Mexican bandits and the Texas Rangers cost the state $200,000." That was the main concern and little was mentioned about the Hispanic suffering and deaths caused by the Rangers.

    Angel Navarro persuaded the bandits to accept defeat, commit no more depredations, and acknowledge that the Lower Rio Grande Valley belonged to Texas," wrote Joseph Dawson. This assertion has been accepted by a number of scholars. The Cortina struggle, however, would continue. Quotes from Joseph Martin Dawson, Jose Antonio Navarro: Co-Creator of Texas (Waco: Baylor University Press, 1969), 97.

37. Canales Interview, June 24,1964. Woodman in his sloppy scholarship, attributed undocumented and questionable utterances to Navarro.

    The journalists and southern patriot Duff Green was also instructed to investigate the Cortina War. See George S. Ulibarri and John P. Harrison, Guide to Materials on Latin America in the National Archives of the United States (Washington: U.S. Government Printing Office, 1987), 44.

38. *Ranchero*, February 25, 1861.

39. Ibid., March 17, 1860. While other Mexicans helped slaves to escape to Mexico, Rodirigo Hinojosa captured two runway Black slaves in Mexico and returned them to their American owners.

40. Ibid.

41. See the title page of the Comisión Pesquisidora.

42. Arthur J. L.Fremantle, The Fremantle Diary: being the journal of Lieutenant Colonel James Arthur Lyon Fremantle, Coldstream Guards, on his three months in the southern states edited by Walter Lord(Boston: Little, Brown, 1954), 9. Previous editions published under title: Three months in the Southern Sates:April-June, 1863 (London: William Blackwood and Sons, 1863), see 22-23.

43. Canales Interview, June 12,1964. Other settlements along the Rio Grande had prosperous Jewish settlements. One of them was El Paso, Texas. Samuel Freudenthal was a prominent a El Paso merchant and civic leader from the 1880s through the Mexican Revolution. See Floyd S. Fierman, Some Early Jewish Settlers on the Southwest Frontier (El Paso: Texas Western College Press, 1960).

44. Fremantle, 11.

CHAPTER VI

Revolution in South Texas

The fighting which took place in Texas following the United States-Mexico War was not the result of banditry as it is often presented nor, for that matter, can it be attributed solely to the activities of the legendary Juan Cortina. Rather, the conflict was deeply social in nature. It was the result of the new Anglo American social order which neglected and violated the rights of *Mexicanos* in the newly occupied territories. Many *Mexicanos* resented and resisted their underclass status as well as the absence of justice and were willing to fight for change.

As poverty and hunger prevailed, the *Cortinista* movement grew, sustained by the struggle against physical brutality, intimidation, destitution, land abuses, and a legal system unwilling or unable to address the complaints of the Mexican population. Most *Mexicanos* were desperately poor and lived in constant fear of losing what little they had. A report from the Mexican government charged: "Mexicans, whether they be Texans or whether they preserve their original nationality, have been victims both in their persons and property, and . . . have not been fully protected by the laws."[1] The report continued by stating that, "Attempts were made to deprive the Mexicans of their lands . . . the cause of which may have been a well-settled principle, leading as far as possible to exclude from an ownership on the soil the Mexicans, whom they (Americans) regarded as enemies and an inferior race."[2] Mexicans witnessed the progressive undermining of their rights under new state laws, which were seen as a vehicle of the ruling class and designed to guarantee their domination of the Texas economy. During the 1850s, frustrations and hatred mounted among the disenfranchised population, and support for Cheno intensified. Canales remembered, desperate people "lit candles to their favorite saints and prayed for anyone to stop the abuses."³

The explosive trigger which led to widespread violence occurred on July 13, 1859. According to Charles Goldfinch, Cortina rode into Brownsville on business and "before returning to his ranch he stopped by Gabriel Catchel's coffee shop."⁴ Here he encountered Marshall Bob Shears "wantonly beat[ing] with the butt of a heavy pistol on the head," of Tomas Cabrera, an old laborer who had worked for Cortina's family and who was being arrested for drunkenness.⁵ Cortina tried to stop Shears, telling him he would take responsibility for the man, "that he knew the ranchero, who was troublesome when drunk, but generally harmless."⁶ Shears responded: "What is it to you, you damn Mexican?" Cortina fired a warning shot and demanded Cabrera's release, and when Shears stood firm, "Cortina shot the Marshall down, took his prisoner, and rode out of town."⁷ (Contrary to myth, Shears survived.) This incident became a catalyst for action, a *cause celebre*, and Cortina became at the same time, a wanted man and a hero; "Cheno" became the symbol of resistance against Anglo control and manipulation.

Author Field Roebuck argued that Shears made a monumental blunder in his handling of this incident. His "reply to "Cheno's" overture started a border war that would last for almost twenty years--a war that would exact its toll in lives and property on both sides of the river." Roebuck added: "He (Cortina) and Bob Shears had accidentally started a miniature revolution, and he simply rode the wave of public sentiment. From his perch, he could not know where the wave would carry him."⁸ For others, like William Neale, an Anglo apologist, "The affair put a feather in Cortina's hat and made him a hero amongst his countrymen; and it was the starting point of his career as a first class thief and cold blooded murderer."⁹

On September 28, 1859, Juan Cortina and a group of followers, who became known as the *Cortinistas*, swept into Brownsville. They searched for their enemies, turned prisoners out of the jail, and threatened to burn the town. The frightened citizens remained indoors while the *Cortinistas*, protesting American injustices, paraded flags and shouted slogans on the streets and in Market Square. Contrary to myth, Cortina's men did not pillage or burn the town.[10] But it was the beginning of a fierce, persistent guerrilla war between Cortina and forces from both the United States Army and the Texas Rangers--a conflict which devastated the lower Rio Grande and cost untold lives. Cortina maintained that he "had entered Brownsville . . . only to bring retribution to those whose punishment had long been delayed." As one report stated, "Lawless and unprincipled Americans were much in the habit of grossly maltreating the Mexicans who visited Brownsville, even to the taking of life."[11] There is no evidence that any plundering took place that night. Of Cortina it was said that "He conducted his campaign against intolerance with the utmost restraint and ruled his men with an iron hand."[12]

Cortina knew his people had lost all faith in the American political system, and he also knew that he was supported by the Mexican population of south Texas. His soldiers had lost land and cattle to the Anglos and they had fought to regain their property and animals.[13] In a late 1859 proclamation he stated:

We have searched the streets of the city for our antagonists, to punish them, since the law is inoperative for them, and justice as administered by them is unfortunately a dead letter. They . . . with a multitude of lawyers, form a band in concert, to dispossess the Mexicans of their lands and afterwards to usurp them.[14]

The Cortina War of 1859

Cortina had organized a regular force of five to six hundred men.[15] Many of those involved in the Cortina War, according to a federal report, were *rancheros* who had been "driven away from the Nueces River."[16] Clearly, wealthy and powerful Texans dreaded these men and the *Cortinista* uprising. Bitterness prevailed and indignation mounted. Judge Israel B. Bigelow wrote in 1859: "The enemy are daily increasing . . . Cortina is making the rancheros believe that this is a revolution, and that he is going to retake the country from the Rio Grande to the Nueces."[17] Anglo landowners William Thomas and Nathaniel White stated:

> *The Mexican population, on both sides of the Rio Grande, is up in arms, with the avowed intention to exterminate every American in the country, and to reconquer it to the Colorado River.*[18]

Thomas and White further concluded:

> *Statements from different quarters force us to conclude that an actual state of war exists on the frontier . . . that Cortina is carrying his lawless and high-handed insurrectionary movements all over the country.*[19]

An urgent call for volunteers went out, with the cry that "the whole of the Rio Grande country is swarming with the robbers of Cortina's party; and all Americans whom they could lay hands on have been killed."[20] In October 1859, following Cortina's raid on Brownsville, frightened Anglo townsmen formed a military organization called the Brownsville Tigers. They sent an expedition against Cortina at Santa Rita, seven miles from Brownsville. It took them a week to reach their destination "and with a display of uniforms and banners they finally drew up in battle array, only to withdraw at almost the first volley from Cortina's men who were hidden in the chaparral. So rapid was the departure of the Tigers that they left their cannon and were in Brownsville in one of the quickest retreats on record."[21] In anger, "an unknown and lawless mob" on November 10, 1859, dragged a 65-year-old man from his place of confinement and hanged him in Market Square, an action which made the local Mexican population even more bitter.[22]

Violent clashes were now common. The *Cortinistas* engaged and defeated the Brownsville Rifles and Tobin's Rangers from San Antonio, and maintained control of the area until the United States Army sent in forces in December, 1859, to crush them. But the *Cortinistas* were simply too large and too well organized to be quickly subjugated. The Cortina rebellion, according to the Army commander, had brought the "depopulation and laying to waste of the whole country from Brownsville to Rio Grande City, 120 miles. Business as far up as Laredo, 240 miles, had been interrupted and suspended for five months."[23] Montejano reports that "there remained no property belonging to Americans that had not been destroyed. And those ranches spared by Cortina's men had been burned by the Texans."[24]

In spite of the damage, the United States government attempted to calm the situation by downplaying the strength of the *Cortinistas* and denouncing their accomplishments. In 1859, General David E. Twiggs noted that he was "disposed to think of the Cortinista affair [as] greatly exaggerated."[25] Other officials dismissed the *Cortinista* strife as a mere race war which should be quickly suppressed. One of the few commentators who perceived the dissension as one of land rather than race was John Haynes. In the state legislature he asked for and argued in favor of a thorough investigation of the revolt. As stated earlier, to Haynes, the dispute was "a deliberate attempt by certain persons to defraud" the Mexicans of their land. Culprits included individuals holding "high official positions in the federal court."[26] Jerry Don Thompson sees Haynes as supportive of Cortina's claim that "a few speculators, assisted by multitudes of lawyers" were endeavoring to "rob the Mexicans of their lands."[27]

Still, the most popular sentiment appeared to favor the total destruction of the *Cortinista* rebellion. On November 19, 1859, a Corpus Christi newspaper stated that the "rebellion must be crushed out and disposed of forever, and Cortina and each and all of his adherent outlaws tracked, caught, and exterminated, and this by the most prompt, energetic and efficient measures."[28] Extremism such as this was intensified when Cortina raided Rio Grande City in December, 1859. Soon thereafter, three Mexicans suspected of being *Cortinistas* were brought to Brownsville and hanged on an old tree. Their bodies were left dangling from the tree for a few days to discourage any future support of Cortina. Yet to the majority of Mexicans, the three Mexicans became saints and martyrs. The manner of their death made them heroes to the *Cortinista* cause.[29]

The 1859 insurrection proved to be just the beginning. Juan Cortina possessed a powerful and attractive ideology and zealous soldiers. The Mexican community along the lower Rio Grande was determined to support Cortina and fight to the last man. Major Samuel P. Heintzelman, who was sent to the Rio Grande to subdue Cortina, wrote on January 29, 1860: "These marauding parties have the active sympathy of all the lower classes of the Mexican population. When Cortina escaped to the other side [Mexico] . . . many small parties were seen, mostly armed. Now they are found at various points, well supplied with arms, ammunition, and supplies, and must be paid from funds obtained from the Mexican population."[30] According to Canales "For Cortina, the people fought tirelessly, silently. Destined to a hard fate, they died without fear. They believed that the resurrection of justice demanded an endless sacrifice of life." An angry Heintzelman aspired to crush every *Cortinista* rebel with extreme ferocity. But he warned again, "Cortinas has the sympathy and aid of the population, and the feeling against the Americans is very great."[31]

The violence soon spilled into Mexican territory. Somehow Cortina's 1859 revolt and his refuge in Mexico in 1860, gave a "pretext for invasion" by John Ford's volunteers in the service of Texas. To gain support for their cause, Ford released a report which stated that after Major Heintzelman first arrived in Brownsville, "Cortina's men captured a government wagon loaded with clothing, killed the driver and mutilated his body in a most shocking manner. According to a report, the clothing was distributed among the outlaws, which saved many of their lives during the fight, the Americans supposing them to be United States Regulars."[32] In reality, it would appear no one really knew who murdered the driver or if there were other victims. Still the local newspaper reported: "Though many Mexicans are firmly adhering to us, none but Mexicans are against us; and the horrible and disgusting mutilation of the bodies of those murdered by Cortina and his co-operators, warn us that instead of a 'Revolution' we are being warred upon by a set of atrocious savages . . . a war upon the American race."[33]

By January 1860, some Americans appeared in Mexico at the Rancho Soledad, near Matamoros. They fired upon families residing there. Then on February 4, the Bolsa Ranch was attacked and burned and several occupants were killed. Later Ford cautioned Mexican "officials against permitting expeditions out of . . . Mexico," that to do so "would be a war in fact, one in which the United States would fight to the end."[34] There was little doubt that those who were suspected of sympathizing with Cortina "were murdered, their families compelled to fly, and their property stolen."[35]

A report released to military authorities at Matamoros declared that Cortina was at the Mesa Ranch and forces were sent in pursuit. Major Heintzelman was notified to be on alert on the American side and troops were alerted in Brownsville and in Edinburg. On the Mexican side, Mexican forces arrived at the Mesa Ranch but did not find Cortina. There twenty-six Mexican troops remained to secure the place. On March 16, Ford and his volunteers attacked the Mexican troops and "some of the soldiers were killed, others dispersed, and the rest made prisoners." Houses were pillaged and the money destined to pay the Mexican soldiers was stolen. After that, Ford and his men continued deeper into Mexico in search of *Cortinistas.* Numerous innocent Mexicans were hanged, especially Elijio Tagle, who denounced their abuses. After stealing horses, Ford and his men recrossed the river into Texas.[36] On April 4, 1860, John Ford crossed into Mexico again at Reynosa. When he went to another settlement, the people, armed and ready, showed themselves on the roofs of the

Juan N. Cortina

houses and on the streets. They told Ford he was surrounded. He responded that he had authority to search for Cortina but the people were suspicious and hostile. Ford quickly returned to Texas.[37] He blamed the whole affair on the "bloodthirsty followers" of Cortina. "It was a self-evident truth that these desperadoes were bent on spilling American blood and plundering American property."[38]

Ford's policy, as well as that of other authorities in Texas, gave strength to Cortina's cause. Cortina reigned supreme. By now the *Cortinistas* had split into different, militant units with boundless confidence to combat their enemies. But the struggle would have to wait as Cortina and the *Cortinistas* would be caught up in an even larger war between the north and the south and in Mexico's struggle for liberation from French occupation.

1.   John Hoyt Williams, Sam Houston: A Biography of the Father of Texas (New York: Simon & Schuster, 1993), 132

2.   Ibid., 129.

3.   Canales Interview, April 15, 1964.

4.   Goldfinch, Cortina, 42.

5.   See United Sates. Army Dept. of Texas, "Difficulties on Southwestern Frontier," 65.

6.   Ibid.; Canales, Juan N. Cortina, 10; Walter Prescott Webb, The Texas Rangers: A Century of Frontier Defense (Austin: University of Texas Press, 1965), 178. Webb wrote, "The unnecessary brutality of the marshall (towards Cabrera) caused Cortina to remonstrate, mildly enough in the beginning. Shears, exasperated at his interference, answered with an insult which called for action. Cortina promptly shot the marshal in the shoulder, took the Mexican (Cabrera)."

7.   Goldfinch, Cortina, 42.

8.   Field Roebuck, "Cheno Cortina: Red Robber of the Rio Grande," True West, (September, 1989), 16. This article is well written, but illustrates the current sloppy scholarship on Cortina.

Another similar article is Russ McDonald, "Notorious Bandito," Wild West, (October, 1993), 42-44. This piece consists of how the "Mexican bandit Tiburcio

Vasquez had grandiose plans to overthrow the *gringos* in California." In some strange way, "Mexican cattlemen at work in South Texas, 1870" became part of the occurrence.

Frequently, university professors write for these magazines, such as University of Oklahoma law professor Robert Barr Smith's article on the Choctaw Nation, "Matter of Honor" in the same issue, 58.

9.   Rayburn and Fray, 65-66. What Neale had to say about Cortina is debatable. "How much of the story bears historical accuracy is a matter of debate. One point is sure, Neale could relate history in a interestingmanner, wrote Bruce Aiken, in "Cheno's Role Depends on Who You Ask," Brownsville *Herald,* May 22, 1992.

10.   Lamar, Readers Encyclopedia, 264.

11.   "Difficulties on Southwestem Frontier," 65.

12.   Goldfinch, Cortina 46; "Difficulties on Southwestern Frontier," 66.

13.   Canales Interview, June 12,1964.

14.   Quoted in Reports of Mexican Border Commission, 132-133.

15.   Montejano, Anglos and Mexicans in the Making of Texas, 32.

16.   Ibid., 32-33.

17.   See letter of Israel B. Bigelow to Editors' News, Brownsville, November 1, 1859, "Difficulties on Southwestern Frontier," 49. Also Corpus Christi *Ranchero,* November 5, 12, 1859.

18.   Affidavit of William D. Thomas and Nathaniel White, San Patricio County, November 6, 1859, in ibid., 50.

19.   Letter, H. Clay Davis, November 3, 1859, in ibid., 51. Also, Brownsville *Ranchero,* November 19, 1859.

20.   Ibid., 58.

21.   Don Graham, intro. The WPA Guide to Texas (Austin: Texas Monthly Press, 1986), 466.

22.   "Difficulties on Southwestem Frontier," 5, 67.

23.   Ibid.; Goldfinch, Cortina, 47; Webb, Texas Rangers, 175-93.

71

24. Ibid.

25. D.E. Twiggs to John B. Floyd, November 17, 1859, in "Difficulties on Southwestern Frontier," 58.

26. Thompson, Vaqueros in Blue & Gray, 86.

27. Ibid.

28. Corpus Christi *Ranchero*, November 19, 1859; January 28, 1860.

29. Frank Cushman Pierce, A History of the Lower Rio Grande Valley (Menasha, Wisconsin: George Banta Publishing Co., 1917), 117; Canales Interview, June 12, 1964.

30. S.P. Heintzelman to W. Seawell, January 29, 1860, "Difficulties on Southwestern Frontier," 106-107.

31. S.P. Heintzelman to the Adjutant General, February 2, 1860, "Difficulties on Southwestern Frontier," 109. See Corpus Christi *Ranchero*, January 7, 1860. The newspaper printed several letters giving details on a battle fought near Rio Grande City between Heintzelman and Cortina. Cortina supposedly lost. One must read these letters with skepticism since Ford was known to gather data for newspapers that fitted his purposes. Also see the *Ranchero*, January 4, 1860. It printed a letter of John Graham to the editor. He stated that Cortina had regrouped at his mothers ranch to do battle with the local authorities. For a comparison see the issue of February 4, 11, 1860. Again Graham noted that Cortina reorganized in Mexico to "lead a war of races along the border."

32. Corpus Christi *Ranchero*, December 24, 1859.

33. Corpus Christi *Ranchero*, December 17, 1859. For details see the *Ranchero*, December 3, 1859. Also see the report on Cortina of the Brownsville *Flag*, November 26, 1859. It commented on the "Proclamation of Juan N. Cortina to the Inhabitants of the State of Texas," November 23, 1859.

34. Ford, Rip Ford's Texas, 289.

35. Reports of the Mexican Border Commission, 195.

36. Ibid., 195-196.

37. Ibid., 196.

38. Ibid., 283.

Juan N. Cortina in uniform
Circa 1864

Juan N. Cortina as civilian
Year Unknown

Estefana Cavazos
Juan N. Cortina's Mother
Circa 1860

Carlos Esparza
Head of the Aguilas Negras
Circa 1870

Santos Benavides
Confederate general who bitterly opposed Cortina
Circa 1870

Young Mexican Confederate Soldier
Circa 1864

4 Mexican Confederate officers from the Laredo area
Circa 1864

A rare and unpublished photograph. One of the few that have survived depict-
ing the tireless, energetic Cortinistas. Four Cortinistas sit in a photographer's
studio in Matamoros about 1865. The two men are dressed in their Cortinista
fieles' uniforms. These uniforms have the Juarista military style. The woman
standing is ElenaVillarreal, a zealous Aguila dama. By her hand, she is show-
ing a gold star as a reward by Cortina for her service. The soldier on the cen-
ter is the tough, brave, combative Martin Arreguin, a leader of several guer-
rilla raids in South Texas. Skilled with explosives, he died shortly after in an
intense battle against the French. The soldier on the right is Esteban, a broth-
er of Elena. The other lady is probably Elena's sister. This tin-type photo like
most of the rest were part of Jose Canales' collection.
Circa 1865

Elena Villareal de Ferrer
Efficient Cortinista spy
Circa 1872

Juan N. Cortina and his young wife Maria
Circa 1891

Panteon de Dolores
Mexico City

Jose Canales
1958

CHAPTER VII

The Cortinistas, the American Civil War and the French Intervention

The Cortinistas and The Confederacy

During the early 1860s, the *Cortinista* struggle for liberation was forced into an even larger conflict, the American Civil War. While Cortina remained committed to his goals and to those of the *Cortinistas*, it was impossible for him to maintain a sense of neutrality. Instead Cortina maneuvered politically between the colossal armies of the North and the South, ever seeking a way to enhance the *Cortinista* interest. The confusing state of affairs resulting from the American Civil War, the French Intervention in Mexico (1861-1867) and the counter attack of the Liberal Army under the Mexican President Benito Juarez tested Cortina's political skill.[1] The political and military leaders of all sides sought the support of Cortina's forces. Pulled in four different directions Cortina nevertheless found a way not just to survive but to become an influential factor in the outcome of the Union, Confederate, Imperialist, and Mexican Liberal military agendas.

In Mexico, Mexican President Benito Juarez escaped to El Paso del Norte, across the Texas border, from the French and Mexican Imperialists.[2] French forces and Mexican Conservatives had installed Maximilian of Austria as Emperor of Mexico in 1864. Cortina assisted Juarez through his control of the Matamoros region and by expediting the flow of arms and supplies to the Liberals under Juarez. In January, 1864, Cortina provided Juarez with 20,000 pesos from

Juan N. Cortina

the Matamoros customhouse, and later sent his brother Jose Maria to Juarez with an additional 25,000 pesos.[3] Also, on January 12, 1864, Cortina "proclaimed himself governor and military commander of the state of Tamaulipas. Because of its locality the region soon became an important key to the success of the opposing armies and Cortina wisely capitalized on this fortune."[4] The Mexican Border Commission later reported:

> *Matamoros, in consequence of the [Union] blockade of the port of Texas, had become a great commercial center for the exportation of cotton and the trade with Texas; its resources amounted to a considerable sum, and they were the only ones at the disposal of the [Juárez] government.[5]*

As historian LeRoy P. Graf noted: "Matamoros was restored to her ancient position as economic capital of the [lower Rio Grande] valley."[6] This was particularly true when it became a vital port for the Confederacy. The city attracted ships from all over Europe, and all imported goods were assessed heavy taxes and freight charges. According to L. Tuffly Elli "Much of the maritime trade through Matamoros was with New York."[7] Between November, 1862 and February, 1863, fifty-nine ships sailed from New York to Matamoros. Unwillingly, the United States Navy cooperated with the city by not having warships at the mouth of the Rio Grande for long periods of time.[8] So important was this Mexican port that S.S. Brown wrote in 1865:

> *Matamoros is to the Rebellion West of the Mississippi what New York is to the United States--its great commercial and financial center, feeding and clothing the rebellion, arming and equipping, furnishing its material of war . . . is a major asset to the Trans-Mississippi area. The entire Confederate Government is greatly sustained by resources from this point.[9]*

Cortinistas, the American Civil War and the French Intervention

Historian James Irby later wrote:

The nations of the world discovered the leak in the Federal Blockade at the Rio Grande in the spring of 1863. All came-- German, Danish, Dutch, French, English, Spanish, and American. Where formerly they had come in twos and threes, they now arrived in squadrons.[10]

Matamoros prevailed as a major port for the Confederacy. "The South had always depended on imports, and by 1863, the Union blockade was so effective that medicines, paper, leather goods, ink, cloth, and toiletries were unavailable."[11] To add to the problem, what goods made it through the blockade doubled in value due to the devaluation of the Confederate dollar.[12]

Juan Cortina knew that Matamoros was financially vital to the Confederacy. For example, Louisiana's Governor Henry Walkins Allen "began collecting sugar and cotton for export to Mexico in exchange for desperately needed ordnance, munitions, dry goods, and machinery." With Cortina's aid, Allen developed a budgetary system that "reestablished an economic stability almost nonexistent elsewhere in the South."[13] With more supplies imported from Mexico, Allen proceeded to aid the Confederate Army. The Union blockade to stop the flow of goods through Matamoros failed. Matamoros was "but another name for Brownsville," protested one indignant Union officer. The blockade was never effective in Texas "so long as unlimited supplies" poured from northern ports into the region by way of the Rio Grande.[14] The *Cortinistas* made themselves indispensable as a matter of monetary survival and encouraged all forms of business to indirectly aid their own cause and kept Matamoros as their headquarters. There "was a good sprinkling of Americans, and the town boasted a commodious market-house, three churches, and a well-built fort on the high bank of the river . . . it seemed quite a metropolis to eyes so long accustomed to the wild solitudes of the frontier."[15]

Now that the Confederacy needed Cortina, he asked the Confederate government to abolish the Committee of Safety which had been organized in Corpus Christi on April 27, 1861. It consisted of fifteen members to protect "the citizens of Nueces County against depredations by Indians, Mexican outlaws and other enemies." In 1861, the committee had attempted to impose its authority to combat "predatory bands of Cortina Mexicans."[16] Canales felt that the committee was little more than a vigilante organization that intended to impose its own concept of law on the Mexican population, but the committee was vigorously supported by Cortina's enemies, such as John Ford, B.F. Neal, John Cannon and others. Therefore, to please Cortina, the Confederate government made the Committee of Safety meaningless.[17]

The Confederacy needed Matamoros to export her cotton and other goods and, in turn, to obtain supplies; to this end they needed Cortina and his army. As William H. Russell wrote in his diary on May 31, 1861, "Cotton is king--not alone king but czar; and coupled with the gratification and profit to be derived from this mighty agency, they look forward with intense satisfaction to the complete humiliation of their hated enemies in the [North]."[18] Due to the Union blockade of the South, the Confederate economic base depended more and more on Matamoros, which Tom Lea called "the back door of the Confederacy."[19] Louisianian A. B. Bacon wrote to Jefferson Davis, "I believe it all important that we should have intimate and most friendly relations with . . . the authorities of Tamaulipas."[20]

Cortina continued to be the major authority in Tamaulipas and an essential ally to the confederates, but the Confederacy also supported Maximilian's Mexico, a fact which disturbed Cortina. Simply stated, a Franco-Confederate military alliance was required to check Yankee aggression on the Rio Grande and so to appease anti-Maximilian forces, the Confederacy promoted Mexican fears of United States greed for more land south of the border.[21] As the Confederate statesman Judah P. Benjamin noted, "The future safety of the Mexican Empire is inextricably bound up with the safety and independence of the Confederacy. Mexico must indulge in no illusion on this point."[22] To inspire the cooperation of Cortina (and to discourage him from joining Union forces), Confederate General John B. Magruder issued Cortina a commission in the Confederate Army and instructed that it be accompanied by a gift of four hundred bales of cotton.[23] As Canales said: "The friendship lasted as long as the Confederacy aided the *Cortinistas* in Texas to promote their civil rights and economic interests."[24] Consequently Cortina pledged that the Confederate flag and individuals seeking protection under it would be ". . . the object of his particular care in Matamoros."[25]

Thus, while Cortina helped Juarez, political expediency eventually required him to "compromise with the French, who were rapidly defeating Juarez's army."[26] Cortina's first concern was with his people's struggle in south Texas. To retain his strength and influence in Matamoros, he had to temporarily look to other interests. Nevertheless, Cortina never abandoned hope that Juarez would oust the French from his country.[27]

The French themselves needed the vital Matamoros trade. Confederate cotton was desperately needed by their weaving industry. Also, munitions and revenues had to be kept from Juarez.[28] As personal physician to Maximilian, Samuel Basch, noted, "In Matamoros, not in the capital [Mexico City], lay the key to the Empire."[29] The French came to consider Cortina their ally and Maximilian even offered him a knighthood. An embarrassed Cortina tried to ignore the honor but did accept the title of honorable officer in Maximilian's army.[30]

Cortina recognized the French "only to gain time and freedom to combat them at the first opportunity," wrote Juan de Dios Arias in 1867.[31] M. Dolan reported on March 2, 1865, " Cortina is still in the service of the Empire, but recruiting fast, and when the time arrives will be found in the right place."[32] The French viewed Mexicans, and the *Cortinistas*, with contempt. French officers appointed and deposed Mexican officials with indifference to their feelings. Canales noted, "The French made Cortina feel inferior because he was a

Mexican and they treated his men shabbily. Still he remained tactful until an opportunity would arise for a rebellion."³³ The opportunity for rebellion against the French came when fortunes changed in the North-South Conflict and Cortina found himself now being courted by Union forces.

The Cortinistas and The Union

Cortina's support for the Confederacy was in no way based on political or philosophical beliefs despite his shift in allegiances. His main objective always was for his movement to survive the turmoil of the American Civil War, and to position himself in the place favorable to the objectives of the *Cortinistas.* To assure this, Cortina had to navigate not only through the changing currents in the war between the North and the South, but also those in the war in Mexico. The key turning point for Cortina in the American Civil War seems to have been the capture of Vicksburg by Union forces. Much to the anger of John Ford and other Confederates, Cortina now expressed a strange preference for the Union. Cortina "established friendly relations with the Union forces, confiscating three of the Kenedy and Company steamships and giving them to Union General N. J. T. Dana for the use of the Federal troops."³⁴ In November 1863, Union General N. P. Banks captured Brownsville and paid an official visit to the American Consul at Matamoros. There, speeches were made by . . . Cortina, and others, expressing their sympathy with the Federal cause in the United States."³⁵

Then, on April 4, 1864, Cortina was honored in Brownsville with a salute, a military review, and a banquet hosted by General Francis Herron. Juan Cortina's friendship with the Union and its military forces was now so amicable that it frightened the Confederacy, and that fear appears justifiable. On April 8, 1864, Major General John A. McClernand interviewed Cortina stating, "adding that he wished to be our friend, and that our success was necessary to the security of Mexico . . . The reply of the Governor is a bold one, amounting to a declaration of war against the rebels, and should it be carried into effect by President Juarez, according to the Governor's recommendation, will be in fact a declaration of war . . . The attitude of the governor . . . appeal strongly to our admiration and gratitude."[36]

Secretary of State William Seward, however, was concerned, indeed nervous about Cortina's friendship. Seward wrote that Cortina's, "presence in arms within the United States in an attitude of war against a friendly power with which the United States are at peace would not be tolerated . . . the neutrality of the United States in the war between France and Mexico" should not be violated.[37] Nevertheless, Seward's comments on Cortina were ignored, and the *Cortinistas* and the Union formed an alliance to help each other.[38] John Ford of the Confederate forces wrote in May of 1865 that there was "an organized band of robbers whose operations extended to both sides of the Rio Grande. . . in communication with the Yankees and possibly . . . in conjunction with them."[39]

French Charge d'affaires M. L. Geofroy observed that "a great number of Federales, after having evacuated Brownsville . . . passed the Rio Bravo and put themselves at the disposal of Mr. Cortinas. The chief would also have received a considerable supply of arms and munitions, dispatched from American territory."[40] Canales affirmed that a large number of Yankees joined the *Cortinistas* against the French and Confederates and that "there must have been a violation of neutrality, which of itself alone would give sufficient ground for reclamation on the part of the Government of the Emperor."[41] It was estimated that in addition to the *Cortinistas* serving under Juarez that there were also 1,200 to 1,500 Americans, many of them black soldiers. An embarrassed United States government refused to acknowledge the black and Anglo Union soldiers in Cortina's forces. Regardless, Cortina continued receiving support and was supplied with materials . . ."[42]

While Seward and others expressed reservations about any involvement with Cortina or the French occupation of Mexico, the

Juan N. Cortina

United States officially opposed the French invasion of Mexico. The Union was particularly worried about French support for the Confederate cause, but the United States government was too preoccupied with its own Civil War to take effective action. Yankee troops could not even enter Mexico without protests from France and England. "General Philip H. Sheridan, concluded that one method of undermining Maximilian was to make overtures to Cortina." "In spite of sharp protest from the French minister, therefore, the army worked rather closely with the Mexican guerrilla leader."[43]

Through Cortina, the federal government hoped to gain control of the lower Rio Grande, and the Union badly needed Cortina to gain a favorable Mexican alliance since most Mexicans bitterly resented the United States. As one Yankee observed : "there is no more affinity between Mexicans and Americans than between oil and water. The natives hate and fear us, and we despise and condemn them. The two races are physically and morally antagonistic . . . it is dislike of the rude, threatening Northmen, and their traditional apprehension that we shall eventually inundate them, destroy their nationality, and overthrow their time-honored customs and their religion."[44]

One way to ensure Cortina support of the Union was to provide him with a steady supply of weapons. Cortina was constantly plagued by a lack of military supplies. Some of his men were even unarmed, and Juarez had no funds to issue rifles nor ammunition to these soldiers who ranged from men to young boys, although a few *Cortinistas* had weapons that had been taken from the French. Washington even offered to make Cortina a general if he would fight in Texas in support of the Union cause.[45] Andrew Hamilton, Military Governor of Texas, toasted Cortina at a Matamoros banquet as a great Union leader, and even went so far as to pledge his support to rid Mexico of the French.[46] Rebel General John B. Magruder wrote on April 27, 1864, that Cortina and Hamilton "walked arm in arm through the streets of Matamoros, and that on that day ten pieces of artillery were formally and officially presented to Governor Cortina by the Federal authorities of Brownsville."[47] The Union aided the

Cortinista "with arms to carry on war against France, whilst they pretend to hold relations of friendship with the latter power."[48] The Union realized fully that the land border between Mexico and Texas had circumvented the blockade. Thus, it desperately wanted to prevent this region from functioning as an avenue for Confederate trade with the outside world since "from the beginning of the war there was great prosperity along the lower Rio Grande."[49] In addition, the Union felt threatened by the consolidation of a powerful Austro-French empire in Mexico, a region rich in minerals. Here again Juan Cortina could be effective to the cause of the Union. Union generals such as Grant went as far as to call for an invasion of Mexico to drive the French out. To General Grant "Mexico seemed an outlet for the disappointed and dangerous elements in the South, elements brave and warlike and energetic enough, and with their share of the best qualities of the Anglo-Saxon character, but irreconcilable in their hostility to the Union."[50] Seward bitterly opposed Grant's ideas, and he and other Union generals urged recognition of Maximilian's government if he rejected the Confederacy and proved his claim of support from the Mexican people.[51] They did not want Maximilian to fall into the arms of the Confederates and for France to become an open ally of the Confederacy.[52] For them, it was absolutely vital that the Union control Cortina if the federal government was to enforce its foreign policy.[53]

All these fears were portrayed vividly by Congressmen such as Senator J. A. McDougall. In 1863, he told the Senate that the French might aid the Confederacy and that they could easily conquer California. "A glance at the map will show that France can land troops and their supplies on the Colorado [River] within five days easy march of San Diego."[54] On May 17, 1865, Grant ordered 25,000 troops to Brownsville for "the purpose of preventing the Confederates from getting aid from Maximilian." Grant hoped it would encourage Liberals such as Cortina to continue resisting the French while at the same time seeking aid from the United States. Grant truly believed "that the [American] Civil War would not be over until the French

Juan N. Cortina

were expelled from Mexico."[55] A scholarly priest, Bernard Doyan justified Grant's preoccupation when he wrote that "Maximilian's Imperialists helped the Confederate troops, whereas Cortina's bandits and other liberals favored the Federals."[56] This was not entirely true, as we have seen, because Cortina had multiple, contradictory allegiances during the 1860s. His overriding motivation was no less than to survive the political turbulence and to use it to continue his people's struggle.[57] Yet while Cortina was able to manipulate the American Generals, he found the task far more difficult with some *Tejanos* who chose to support different sides in the American Civil War. For example, *Cortinistas* were confronted with *Tejanos* who joined the Confederacy, and, according to Jose Canales, "To attack the Tejano Confederates was to destroy themselves. Most Tejanos believed that to get rid of Uncle Sam was to solve their problem of oppression. The Confederacy, for some strange reason, seemed to offer them equal rights. At least they thought that."[58] Despite alliances, Cortina did not care for either side. Juan Cortina believed that the Civil War would only last about four years so he remained calm. Cortina believed it might be counter-productive to attack Hispanic leaders such as Colonel Santos Benavides of the Confederate Army. He gave strict orders to the *Fieles*, one of Cortina's militant units, and other *Cortinistas* to avoid combat with the Confederates unless he personally approved it. Cortina believed the Confederates and their cause would eventually be destroyed.

Earlier, Cortina had himself engaged in battle with the Confederate forces under Benavides. After that, however, he cooperated with him to avoid any unnecessary friction in the Hispanic community. This is exemplified in a letter that Major General John B. Magruder wrote to Cortina on May 22, 1864 stating, "It gives me pleasure to express to you my gratification at learning that you have made arrangements with Colonel Benavides . . . to protect the cotton trade across the Mexican border by way of Laredo."[59] At the end of 1864 Cortina went as far as to "send him [Benavides] Christmas greetings and several bottles of French wine. It was a cheap price to

82

pay to keep Benavides from depleting Cortinista resources with petty, armed conflicts. This way Cortina could apply his energy and resources to major important issues."[60] A discreet Cortina remained unruffled. He knew that Benavides and the Confederacy's days were numbered.

In the end Cortina was correct. The south succumbed to the north and the American Civil war came to an end in 1865. Nevertheless, the French occupation of Mexico continued and the enduring struggle for justice in Texas was far from over. For Cortina and his followers the struggle continued.

The Cortinistas and the French Intervention in Mexico

Just as he had played an important role in the American Civil War, Cortina was a significant factor in the development and outcome of the French Occupation of Mexico. Ousted President, Benito Juarez, and his exiled government depended heavily on Cortina and his supporters to collect much needed revenues for his cause. Deep roots of friendship existed between Cortina and the Mexican President since Juarez's period of exile in New Orleans. As early as the 1850s, Juarez depended upon Brownsville for one thing or another, and Cortina's family and friends constantly provided needed aid to Juarez and his supporters, such as Melchor Ocampo, who lived in Brownsville for some time.[61]

Throughout the occupation, Cortina's *Fieles* were needed to guard the roads and keep the avenues of communication open with the Mexican president.[62] They also provided Juarez's cohorts, such as Matias Romero, with sanctuary in Matamoros.[63] It was through Matamoros that the *Cortinistas* were able to supply the forces of Benito Juarez with medical supplies such as quinine, opium, calomel, chloroform and iodine. Early in the conflict, President Juarez encouraged Cortina and his *Fieles* to guard and promote Matamoros as a market for a lucrative Confederate-European trade in order to obtain revenues. Union diplomats were ignored in requesting use of

83

the "territory of Mexico for moving troops from California against Texas." President Juarez was reported to have refused the Union's request on the grounds that "Mexico was too small a power to incur the enmity and hostility of either of the American belligerents."[64]

Publicly, Juarez and Cortina sided with the Confederacy, but this was only a relationship of convenience. They never trusted the Confederacy, because it consisted of Texans and other southerners, who had designs on Mexican territory. When their allegiance did change to favor the Union, the Confederate emissary, J.T. Pickett "became belligerent and tactless, threatening the Mexican government with an invasion of Confederate troops."[65] For Cortina and Juarez, however, the French advance and not Confederate threats was the more pressing issue.

On June 26, 1864, Union General F. J. Herron reported that "the Juarez government is gradually dying out, judging from appearances, and the people seem to be willing to have any kind of a ruler if the war will cease. The French, under Du Pris [Dupin], had occupied Victoria, the capital of Tamaulipas. Cortina with 500 men and six pieces of artillery, is on his way to meet them, but will not do anything. He was at last account about 115 miles from Matamoros, moving toward Victoria."[66] Charles Dupin had been "named as provisional governor of Tamaulipas from 1864 to 1865."[67] Disliked by Maximilian because of his crudeness, he was ordered north "to organize the regiment of counter-guerrillas."[68] The main purpose of this counter-guerrilla unit was for Dupin to destroy the *Cortinista* guerrillas and *Juarista* Liberals, and, at first, it appeared that he might do just that.[69]

Shortly after Cortina left Matamoros, two French war vessels appeared at the mouth of the Rio Grande, prompting Cortina to ask General Herron to assist him. He wrote, "This case is one of necessity, and interests both nations, for if the French and the traitors should occupy the state, especially this frontier, the consequences would perhaps be fatal to the cause which you defend and which the United States uphold."[70] Herron who had personal differences with

Cortina ignored the request leaving the *Cortinistas* to their fate. Historian Gabriel Saldivar recorded that Cortina "with his battalion of Fieles of Tamaulipas," battled the French forces of Charles Dupin.[71] Cortina instructed his *Fieles* to use guerrilla tactics since they lacked ammunition and other military supplies, but his tactics failed, and for the first time, Cortina faced defeat.

During the French occupation of Tamaulipas Charles Dupin more than lived up to his reputation for barbarity, using prisoners for his cruel games. Most were hanged from trees or from city lamp posts, while others were cut in half. Captured *Fieles* and other *Cortinistas* were actually singled out for this treatment.[72] Dupin would later declare: "When you kill a Mexican that is the end of him. When you cut off an arm or a leg, that throws him upon the charity of his friends, and then two or three must support him. Those who make corn can not make soldiers. It is economy to amputate."[73] When Dupin maimed and mutilated the *Fieles* soldiers, he refused to use chloroform or wine in order that the victim would suffer more. According to Justo Sierra, "Tamaulipas, martyrized by Dupin's vandals, was overrun."[74] The French leader's actions, however, only motivated other Mexicans to join Cortina and fight the French.[75]

One of Dupin's fiercest enemies was Pedro Mendez, a *Fiel* officer. According to Jasper Ridley, Mendez distributed "stirring propaganda leaflets" in the path of French forces. At the end of November 1864, he was active near Victoria. On one occasion as Dupin's forces fought the *Cortinistas*, Dupin located the corpses of collaborators and several French soldiers hanging from trees. He later discovered a newly dug grave in the middle of the road and on it was a cross to which a notice was attached: "Death to the French murderers!" One exasperated counter-guerrilla ripped down the cross and the notice. "As he touched it, a bomb exploded, killing him, and as his startled comrades ran for cover, Mendez's men opened fire on them from their hiding place beside the road."[76] Dupin survived the attack and proceeded, "to commit all kinds of atrocities."[77] He would eventually be "recalled for his cruelty . . . and replaced by . . . another French officer."[78]

Cortina's military losses also meant he had lost his position as governor. President Juarez bemoaned Cortina's loss of Matamoros which had been so vital to his cause. According to Joan Haslip, "The capture of Matamoros and of Monterrey had forced Juarez to seek refuge in the deserts of Chihuahua, while a successful assault on Tampico had brought another gulf port into French hands and assured a second lifeline to Europe."[79] Nevertheless, as governor of Tamaulipas, Cortina still used "the port of Tuxpan, where blockade runners brought the Juaristas supplies from the United States and from Havana."[80]

One of Cortina's more serious defeats came at the hands of the Imperial General Tomas Mejia. Yet despite Cortina's defeat and the eventual French occupation of Matamoros, Cortina still had the upper hand in the region. For example, General Sheridan reported on July 10, 1865, that "Nearly all the people out of Matamoros are Liberals, and the majority of those within the city. The French soldiers are deserting, and there is generally a very uneasy state of affairs with the authorities."[81] According to Canales even the French troops who had deserted were joining *Cortinista* units such as the *Exploradores*.[82] The *Exploradores* was yet another one of Cortina's units whose principal task was to patrol the Rio Grande River and the shallow banks near Port Isabel. They used their own vessels, such as pilot and fishing boats and merchant craft to attack all their enemies whether they be French, Union, or Confederates.

French defections and Liberal support for Cortina and the *Juaristas* weakened Tomas Mejia, a general in Maximilian's army, and the French command, a situation recognized by General Sheridan: "The French authorities are very much embarrassed. Cortina drives in Mejia's pickets at pleasure." [83] To add to Mejia's problems Cortina held "all the roads around Matamoros. Says he could take the place if he had ammunition...[He] Has, as governor of Tamaulipas under the Liberal government, given permission for our [Union] forces to enter

Mexico."[84] Mejia desperately wanted to capture and execute Cortina and thereby destroy the invincibility of the *Cortinistas* once and for all. However, the tide had turned and it was now Cortina's turn to win. With his *Exploradores* Cortina joined other *Juaristas* and continued to torment Mejia and the French forces "and hovered like vultures on their trails."[85] When Mejia finally evacuated Matamoros, Cortina again assumed the governorship.[86] He quickly took control of his beloved Matamoros, the heart of the *Cortinista* structure, and found it to be still beating, vibrant and strong. Its arteries were again throbbing with the flow of new recruits, precious munitions and cherished supplies.

Cortina's victory, together with others led, in the end, to the expulsion of the French from Mexico. By December 1866, French troops began to leave Mexican soil, followed by the executions of Maximilian and Mejia at Queretaro on June 19, 1867. Juan Cortina and his forces had done their part to ensure that Mexico would remain an independent nation, but to do so meant that Cortina had to place his own struggle on hold in order to support an even larger cause. Cortina had wanted his struggle to survive at all cost, yet he had made certain that Juarez received the tax revenues from numerous parts of Tamaulipas.[87]

Following the French Occupation, Cortina lived continually in Mexico becoming increasingly active in politics south of the border. He would eventually be moved in 1877 to central Mexico, where his activities could be monitored by newly-elected President Porfirio Diaz, who was wary of Cortina's power and independence. Diaz was particularly concerned about Cortina's activities north of the Rio Grande and how they might affect United States-Mexican relations. For their part Cortina's forces remained loyal to him well after the hostilities of the 1860s and were ready to continue with the old struggle. According to Canales, they crossed the Rio Grande to fight the Texas Rangers or United States Army troops "to obtain food, supplies, or revenues of which they were always in need." He adds, "A *curandero* with a talking cross accompanied the troops for spiritual and moral support. Another *curandero* carried a banner, portraying the Virgin of Guadalupe."[88]

The Mexican Border Commission referred to the *Fieles* in 1873 as "adventurers from both frontiers" and lamented that "many people of the worst reputation joined."[89] The Commission further claimed that the *Fieles* were "men undisciplined and immoral, and who remained but a short time in Cortina's service. They frequently deserted, stealing both the horse they rode and their arms . . . and returned to their previous life of crime and robbery."[90] Cortina, however, had a dramatically different view of his men. According to Canales, "Cortina reflected a boundless confidence in his *Fieles* and *Exploradores*. Their hats and colorful ribbons shadowed their faces, adding suspense to the soldiers. One could barely see their sorrow or hunger or their tormented souls. The majority of these unknown soldiers endured Cortina's political adjustments and the grotesque elements of the era: hardships, privation, illness and at times a quick, violent death."[91]

Fanny Chambers Gooch best described the social, economic and political climate of the border region when she wrote around 1881: "The antagonism between the United States and Mexico is unquestionably more largely due to border troubles than to any other cause . . . considering the causes that exist for unfriendly feeling, the difficulties that occur on the Rio Grande are not remarkable. The floating, unsettled population drift to both borders, and the magistracy on both sides is feeble."[92]

The pragmatic Porfirio Diaz offered to bring peace to the Rio Grande frontier, ending heavy losses to cattle barons such as King and Kenedy. He promoted an economic program that linked Mexico to the United States through railroads, major foreign investments and by selling Mexican mineral rights to the outside world. Diaz supporters called themselves "Railroaders," and even a pro-Diaz newspaper was named *The Railroader*.[93] Diaz brought together Mexican laissez-faire liberals, provincial elites who saw prosperity in the railroads, Texas entrepreneurs, New York bankers and other foreign merchants.

Cortina, however, endured as an obstacle to all this. He and his followers wanted to continue to fight for what they felt was rightfully theirs.

1. James A. Irby, Backdoor at Bagdad: The Civil War on the Rio Grande, (El Paso, Texas Western Press, 1977), 29-41: Reports of Mexican Border Commission, 151-153.

2. Williams, With the Border Ruffians, 433-34.

3. Douglas, "El Caudillo de la Frontera," 82; Stambaugh, Lower Rio Grande Valley, 108.

4. Reports of Mexican Border Commission, 150, 152.

5. Ibid., 151.

6. LeRoy P. Graf, "The Economic History of the Lower Rio Grande Valley, 1820-1875." Ph.D. dissertation, Harvard University, 1942, 589. Also Jose T. Canales, "Cotton and Guns: Brownsville During the Civil War," in Reflections from the Collected Papers of the Lower Rio Grande Valley Historical Society, 1949-1979 (Harlingen: Lon C. Hill Memorial Library, 1979), 93-95.

7. L. Tuffy Ellis, "Maritime Commerce on the Far Western Gulf, 1861-1865," and Marilyn McAdams Sibley, "Charles Stillman: A Case Study of Entrepreneurship on the Rio Grande 1861-1865," Southwestern Historical Quarterly (October 1973), 206.

8. Ibid., 205.

9. U.S. War Department, The War of the Rebellion: A Compilation of the Official Records of the Union and Confederate Armies (Washington, D.C.: Government Printing Office, 1880-1901), Series 1, Volume 48, Part 1, 512-13. This 130-volume compilation is a valuable major resource on Cortina. Hereafter referred to as O. R Also Ellis, "Maritime Commerce on the Far Western Gulf," 167-240.

    Matamoros reached its economic peak in May, 1865. After May, real estate in the city collapsed. Several landlords were refusing $8,000 a year rent in advance for newly constructed buildings. By the end of the year they were fortunate if they could get $800 a year. See Tri-Weekly Telegraph (Houston), May 19, June 2, 1865.

10. Irby, Backdoor to Bagdad, 27. Also Robert W. Delaney, "Matamoros, Port for Texas during the Civil War," Southwestern Historical Quarterly (April 1955), 473. Also, Gilbert D. Kingsbury, "Description of Brownsville and its Trade (1865?)," Gilbert D. Kingsbury Papers, Barker Texas History Center.

Juan N. Cortina

11. Anderson and Anderson, 315.

12. Ibid., 315-316.

13. Patricia L. Faust, ed., Historical Times Illustrated Encyclopedia of the Civil War (New York: Harper & Row, 1986), 70.

14. Marilyn McAdams Sibley, "Charles Stillman: A Case Study of Entrepreneurship on the Rio Grande, 1861-1865," Southwestern Historical Quarterly (October 1973), 233.

15. Williams, With the Border Ruffians, 279.

16. Ranchero, May 3, 1861.

17. Canales Interview, April 12,1964.

18. William Howard Russell, My Diary North and South (Boston: T. 0. H. P. Burnham, 1863), 251. See the farcical sketch, "The Naval Army or a Blow in the Rear," Frank Leslie's Illustrated Newspaper, November 9, 1881. The sketch attempts to illustrate the importance of cotton to the Confederacy. Also in this same issue, December 28, 1861, is the sketch of a puzzled "John Bull" while the African "Nigger" is holding cotton on his head and an African "Nigger" is without.

19. Tom Lea, The King Ranch (Boston: Little, Brown & Company, 1957), 1:183. "Cotton is King in Matamoros and Bagdad," concluded the New York Herald, January 9,1865. Some cotton was lost due to "stupid (Confederate] officers" and "ill-advised and improper proceedings," noted the San Antonio Semi-Weekly News, July 17,1862.

20. A.B. Bacon to Jefferson Davis, November18, 1861, "Proceedings of the Confederate Congress," Southern Historical Society Papers, Vol. XXIV (Richmond: Virginia Historical Society, 1923-1959). Also, Thomas David Schoonover, Dollars Over Dominion: The Triumph of Liberalism in Mexican - United States Relations, 1861-1867 (Baton Rouge: Louisiana State University Press, 1978), 13-47.

21. Blumberg, The Diplomacy of the Mexican Empire, 17.

22. Ibid; See also Colonel John S. Ford to Acting Assistant Adjutant General, Lieutenant W. Keamey, Brownsville, Texas, August 26, 1864; Captain A. Veron, Corps expeditionnaire de la marine Francais a Bagdad, Mexico, August 25,1884; Colonel J.J. Fisher to Colonel John S Ford, August 27, 1864; General Juan N. Cortina to Colonel John S. Ford, Matamoros, Mexico, September 8, 1864; Colonel John S. Ford to Colonel J.N. Cortina, Brownsville, Texas, September 8,1864. All these documents are in the Ford Military Correspondence, Daughters of the Confederacy Museum, Austin. These cited archives deal with the French attitude toward the Confederacy, primarily in Matamoros.

23. Reports of Mexican Border Commission, 152; 0 R 1, 34 Pt. 3: 87.

24. Canales Interview, June 9,1964.

25. Captain A. Veron, Corps expeditionaire de la marine Francais a Bagdad, Mexico, August 25, 1864 and Colonel J.J. Fisher to Colonel John S. Ford, August 27, 1864 in Ford Military Correspondence.

26. Graf, "Economic History of the Lower Rio Grande Valley," 589.

27. Canales Interview, June 9, 1964.

28. Irby, Backdoor to Bagdad, 26-30.

29. Samuel Basch, Memories of Mexico: A History of the Last Ten Months of the Empire, trans. by Hugh McAden Oechler, (San Antonio: Trinity University Press, 1973), 172-73.

30. Canales Interview, June 9,1964. The major reason that the French honored Cortina was as Samuel Basch, personal physician to Maximilian, stated, "In Matamoros, not in the capital, lay the key to the (Maximilian) empire." Bash, Memories of Mexico, 173.

Maximilian made Cortina a knight of the Order of Guadalupe [Orden de Guadalupe] in the summer of 1865. Cortina also received the Order of the Mexican Eagle [Orden del Aguila Mexicana]. Years later Cortina gave Canales the medals. Canales later gave me these items.

Cortina could not wear them and was embarrassed to show them. Although Cortina officially tried not to acknowledge the honors from Maximilian, he was afraid to offend Juarez. In trying to hold on to the Matamoros area, Cortina was constantly caught between Maximilian and Juarez.

Felipe Berriozabal, a rival of Cortina, told Canales that he saw these medals at Cortina's headquarters. Unfortunately, most of the records pertaining to these orders have been lost. Albert S. Evans, Our Sister Republic: A Gala Trip Through Tropical Mexico in 1869-1870 (Hartford: Columbian Book Co., 1870), 312-16. Also, Frank W. Grove, Medals of Mexico: Orders. Awards and Military Decorations (New York: Privately Published, 1974), 16-20.

Canales had the original "Registro de Cruces y Comendcoraciones Mexicanos," a listing of all awards, even issues prior to the French Intervention. It appears from this document that the empire issued past-due Republic medals. There are 464 listings. It has a cover stamped with the Imperial seal of the "Secretaria de Estado y Negocios Estanjeros," (1864).

Juan N. Cortina

Canales had the original "Registro de Cruces y Comendcoraciones Mexicanos," a listing of all awards, even issues prior to the French Intervention. It appears from this document that the empire issued past-due Republic medals. There are 464 listings. It has a cover stamped with the Imperial seal of the "Secretaria de Estado y Negocios Estanjeros," (1864).

Canales also gave me the "Gran Cancilleria de las Ordenes Imperiales" (August 25,1866) listing what awards were made and to whom. Such awards as the Order of the Mexican Eagle, the Order of Guadalupe, the Order of San Carlos, and the Cross of Preservance are included.

31. Juan de Dios Arias, Reseña Historia de Ejército del Norte durante la Intervención Francesa (Mexico: Imprenta de Nabor Chávez, 1867), 31.

32. M. Dolan to Stephen A. Hurlbut, March 2, 1865, O.R., XVIII: 1,1058.

33. Canales Interview, June 27,1964.

34. Keamey and Knopp, Boom and Bust, 131. Also Cortina felt uneasy about an "alliance between the French and the Confederates for the purpose of attacking us, and given us cause to take the precautionary measures adopted at this post." Quote from General Juan N. Cortina to Colonel John S. Ford, Matamoros, Mexico, September 8, 1884, Ford Military Correspondence.

35. Frazar Kirkland, Anecdotes and Incidents of the Rebellion (Hillsdale, Michigan: W.E. Allen & Co., 1888), 142.

36. John A. McClenand to N.P. Banks, April 8, 1864, O.R., I, XXXIV, 2: 87-88.

37. William H. Seward to E.R.S. Canby, September 30, 1864, 0 R I XLI 3: 497-498.

38. Colonel John S. Ford to Acting Adjutant General, Captain J. E. Dwyer, Brownsville, Texas, September 3, 1864, Ford Military Correspondence. In this document, Ford wrote about Cortina, "He hates Americans; particularly Texans.... He knows his career is nearly closed. If he could force his way through our lines, plunder our people, and get within the Yankee lines, it would [be] a finale he would delight in."

39. J. .S. Ford to Tomás Mejia, May 28,1865, U.S. Congress, House Executive Document, 39th Congress, 1st Session, no.73, "The Conditions of Affairs in Mexico," 1, no.48 (Washington D.C.: Government Printing Office, 1866), 528.

40. L. De Geofroy to William H. Steward, August 27, September 23, 1864, "The Conditions of Affairs in Mexico," II, 314, 316.

Cortinistas, the American Civil War and the French Intervention

41. Translation of French memorandum enclosed with F.W. Steward to E. M. Stanton, August 29, 1864, <u>O.R.</u>, I, XLI, 2: 916.

42. Canales Interview, June 24, 1964.

43. A. Russell Buchanan, <u>David S. Terry of California: Dueling Judge</u> (San Marino: The Huntington Library, 1956), 140. See also Lieutenant-Colonel G. H. Giddings to Colonel John S. Ford, Camp Palmito, Texas, September 11, 1884, and Colonel John S. Ford, report of September 30, 1884, in part damaged, probably to General Drayton or Slaughter in Ford Military Correspondence.

44. Anonymous American, <u>Maximilian and the Mexican Empire: Non-Intervention the True Policy of the United States</u> (New York: Sackett & Mackay, Law Printers, 1866), 7.

45. Canales Interview, August 12,1964; Also, Ford, <u>Rip Ford's Texas</u>, 375, and New Orleans *Picayune*, February 9, 1864.

46. New Orleans *Picayune*, April 27,1864; John L, Waller, <u>Colossal Hamilton of Texas: A Biography of Andre Jackson Hamilton</u> (El Paso: Texas Western Press, 1968), 52-53.

47. J.B. Magruder to John Slidell, April 27, 1864, <u>O R</u> 1, XXXIV, 3: 796.

48. Ibid.

49. Stambaugh, <u>Lower Rio Grande Valley</u>, 111-112.

50. Quoted in Young, 164.

51. Blumberg, <u>Diplomacy of the Mexican Empire</u>, 18.

52. Schoonover, <u>Dollars Over Dominion</u>, 30-35.

53. Canales Interview, June 12,1964.

54. J.A. McDougall, <u>French Interference in Mexico in the Senate of the United States on Tuesday, February 3rd,1863</u> (Baltimore: John Murphy & Co., 1863), 24, 28.

55. Stambaugh, <u>Lower Rio Grande Valley</u>, 127.

56. Bernard Doyon, <u>The Cavalry of Christ of the Rio Grande, 1849-1883</u> (Milwaukee: Catholic Life Publications, 1956), 168.

Juan N. Cortina

57. Canales Interview, August 12,1964. For a political account of that era in relation to Mexico see: Brownsville El Zaragoza, December 27,1865. For a comparison see Harper's Weekly, March 23,1861.

58. Canales Interview, June 12.1964.

59. J.B. Magruder to Juan N. Cortina, May 22, 1864, O.R., I, XXXIV, 3: 835.

60. Canales Interview, June 12,1964.

61. Canales Interview, June 28,1964. For Ocampo in Brownsville, see: Ralph Roeder, Juarez and His Mexico, (New York: Viking Press, 1947) 110-111, 113.

62. Canales Interview, June28, 1964.

63. Romero stayed in Matamoros during September, 1863. See Gorham D. Abbot, Mexico and the United States: Their Mutual Relations and Common Interests (New York: G.P. Putnam 7 son, 1869), 181; Canales Interview, June 28, 1964.

64. Ibid., 323-324.

65. Alvin M. Josephy, The Civil War in the American West (New York: Alfred A. Knopf, 1992), 56. Canales Interview, June 28,   1964.

66. F.H. Herron to William Dwight, June 26, 1864, 0 R I XXXIV, 4: 560.

67. Pierce, A Brief History, 56.

68. Edwin Adams Davis, Fallen Guidon: The Forgotten Saga of General Jo Shelby's Confederate Command, The Brigade that Never Surrendered and its Expedition to Mexico (Santa Fe: Stagecoach Press, 1962), 99.

69. Canales Interview, November 16, 1964.

70. J.N. Cortina to F.J. Herron, June 21, 1864, ibid.

71. Gabriel Saldivar, Historia Comprendiada de Tamaulipas, (Mexico: Academia Nacional de Historia y Geografia, 1945), 229.

72. Ibid. Pierce mentions some of the hangings. Pierce, A Brief History, 56. For more cruelties, see: Davis, Fallen Guidon, 100.

73. Quoted in Davis, Fallen Guidon, 100.

74.   Justo Sierra, The Political Evolution of the Mexican People (Austin: University of Texas Press, 1969), 327.

75.   Canales Interview, November 16, 1964; Davis, Fallen Guidon, 100.

76.   Ridley, Maximilian and Juarez, 193; Keratry, 241, 270-271,   274.

77.   Saldivar, 231. See Juan Manuel Torrea, Estado de Tamaulipas: Diccionario Geografico, Historico, Biografico y Estadistico de la Republica Mexicana (Mexico: Sociedad Mexicana de Geografica y Estadistica, 1940), 279-280; Keratry, 177-180.

78.   Hubert Howe Bancroft, The Works of Hubert Howe Bancroft, Vol. XIV, History of Mexico: (San Francisco: The History Co., 1888), 6:197. See footnote 35. Also see Arias, Reseña Historica, 55-56 and primarily 73.

79.   Joan Haslip, The Crown of Mexico: Maximilian and His Empress Carlota (New York: Holt, Rinehart and Winston, 1971), 278.

80.   Dabbs, French Army in Mexico, 85.

81.   P.H. Sheridan to [Ulysses S.] Grant, July 10, 1865, O.R., I, XVIII, 2:1067.

82.   Canales Interview, June 24,1964.

83.   P.H. Sheridan to [Ulysses S.] Grant, July 10, 1865, O.R., I, XVIII, 2: 1067.

84.   P.H. Sheridan to U.S. Grant, July 10, 1865, in ibid.

85.   Dabbs, French Army in Mexico, 175; Bazaine's secretary to Bazaine, Telegram No.465, July 25, 1866, in Bazaine Archives, XXII, 4, 341.

86.   Saldivar, Historia Tamaulipas, 315-316.

87.   Ibid., 228. Canales Interview, November 16, 1964.

88.   Canales Interview, June 12,1964. During this era, the *Cortinistas* admired the legendary Nicolas Romero, leader of the Michoacan guerrillas. He championed the poor against the rich. Like Cortina, his support came from the lower classes and from middle-class liberals. Like numerous *Cortinistas*, young men left their homes in several Mexican towns to join Romero. According to Canales, Romero's forces and Cortina's followers helped each other since they were *Juaristas*.

89.   Reports of Mexican Border Commission, 154; Ford, Rip Ford's Texas, 274-276.

90.   Ibid., 155. The commission failed to mention that most of Cortina's men were disciplined and had devoted their lives to the cause. Yet Cortina needed brutal men to deal with the abuses of the Rangers.

As N.A. Jennings wrote about the Ranger visits to Matamoros after nightfall: "We went there for two reasons: to have fun, and to carry out a set policy of terrorizing the Mexicans at every opportunity." Captain McNelly wanted his men to be feared as to gain a reputation "as fire-eating, quarrelsome dare-devils as quickly as possible" to assert themselves over the "Greasers." Jennings, A Texas Ranger, 141-143. "The Mexicans were afraid of us, collectively and individually, and added to the fear was a bitter hatred," Jennings said.

As for some of Cortina's men being "undisciplined and immoral," it should be noted that such was also a common problem in the Union and Confederate armies during the Civil War. "Verbal assaults were sometimes overlooked, but it was impossible to ignore a physical attack on an officer." To enforce discipline, there were numerous punishments and "a great deal of inequity in sentencing and, consequently, much resentment among the troops." James I. Robertson, The Civil War: Tenting Tonight. The Soldier's Life (Alexandria: Time-Life, 1984), 65.

91.   Canales Interview, August 15, 1964. With his *Fieles*, Cortina remained active in Matamoros. Although the Brownsville *Ranchero* does not mention the *Fieles*, it reported the *Cortinistas* activities in Matamoros. See the *Ranchero* issues of November 28, December 1, 2, 7, 8, 13, 14, 20 and 21.

92.   Fanny Chambers Gooch, Face to Face with the Mexicans, ed. C. Harvey Gardiner (Carbondale: Southern Illinois University Press 1966), 246.

93.   Hart, Revolutionary Mexico, 117.

CHAPTER VIII

The Aguilas Negras,
Spies and Terror

One of Juan Cortina's major assets was his ability to gain support for his cause through the creation of a military organization. Cortina's military units were instrumental in the realization of his objectives and were influential in the American Civil War and the French Occupation of Mexico. These military units continued to confront the American political structure well into the 1870s. While many like General Edward O. C. Ord and other military and political figures resented Cortina's men, merchants in Matamoros, Brownsville, and in other areas, were grateful to Cortina for protecting, if not promoting, their economic interests.

One important group that Cortina organized was the *Aguilas Negras*. Directed by Carlos Esparza, they were Cortina's policemen and spies. Cortina depended on them for his successful surprise attacks. With a blind allegiance to Cortina, the *Aguilas* also served as guides and scouts because they were intimately familiar with the region, covered with woods, swamps, obscure roads and cow-paths; In short, they knew their way through the dense undergrowth and the dark ravines. This particular organization remained so secretive, however, that no one is certain of its official name or if it even had one.[1] Some have even dismissed the existence of such a group as a myth. Twentieth century historians such as Rodolfo Acuña and Arnoldo de Leon have been frustrated by their inability to find other historical documentation for the name *Aguilas*.[2] However, a few fragmented oral narratives in the form of *corridos* (ballads) about the

Aguilas have survived into the twentieth century. These sources together with the memoirs of Jose T. Canales as well as accounts of local residents might help bring clarity to this issue. These sources, while limited, suggest that such an organization did in fact exist. Our conclusions, therefore, rely heavily on Canales' work.

Canales himself was not entirely sure of the origin of the name *Aguilas*. He believed they may have been named after the daring Cuban *Aguilas,* a secret revolutionary society which plotted independence in that country in the 1820s. Canales also suspected that a group of Cuban exiles may have belonged to the Cortina unit. Of the group, Canales commented, "They had a talent to camouflage themselves and quickly disappear into the Mexican population. That was their basic strength to survive and baffle their enemies. How could their antagonists destroy them if they did not know who to fight?"[3] Canales asserted that the *Aguilas'* activities and affiliations sometimes overlapped those of other *Cortinista* groups, the *Fieles* and *Exploradores*, and for this reason they were difficult to identify.

According to Canales they would ride at night, preferably after midnight, to search for their foes. To their rivals they were devils from the "depths of hell bringing terror." As Canales stated, "One never knew who the next victim was. To their friends, they were the black knights or angels who rode at night to enforce justice."[4] He continued, "It must have been sheer terror to see these elongated, black figures. They covered their faces in monk's cowls attached to their gowns. They created an infinite horror to their enemies with their deadly silence and lethal movements to defend themselves in a world of hatred and contempt."[5]

Canales further argued that at one time the *Aguilas* were spies during the Mexican War for the *Defensores de la Patria*, 1844 -1851.[6] While camping opposite Matamoros, Lieutenant John C. Peck wrote on April 16, 1846, "Our camp is full of (Mexican) spies."[7] In fact, Juan Cortina himself served as a soldier and later as an informant during the war and was head of the organization which at that time consisted of Mexican Indians.[8]

Samuel Reid, a contemporary, observed, "The Americans make very good spies . . . but the Mexicans excel them . . . the Indians are superior to either. The keen perception, circumspection, untiring patience and self-denial, and indomitable perseverance so absolutely essential to success, the Indians possess such an extraordinary degree, that they seem fitted by nature to the task."[9] William A. Neale, who lived in Brownsville, was probably describing the *Aguilas* when he asserted: "Cortina was informed about the movements amongst our citizens through the spies that he had amongst our tame Mexicans. So well were these spies organized, that the very morning the secret orders were given for the company [of Anglo army volunteers] to move, Cortina was informed in less than a quarter of an hour."[10]

During the Civil War when Confederates depended on the Rio Grande and Matamoros to export cotton, the *Aguilas* centered their operations in Matamoros and Bagdad, near the mouth of the Rio Grande on the Mexican side. Canales stated "It is Bagdad where they may have kept what records they had. It also served as a recruiting and training center for guerrilla warfare."[11] They enlisted men from the local population, which consisted of "Americans, Spaniards, Italians, French, Germans, Greeks and, really least of all, Mexicans."[12] Canales believed, these foreigners shared an economic interest, such as trade and import revenues with the *Cortinistas*.

On June 22, 1864, the *Aguilas* renamed Bagdad, *"Villa Cortina"* and named one of the *Aguila* officers, Jose Maria Vidal Millan as the mayor.[13] British officer Arthur J. L. Fremantle noted: "Bagdad consists of a few miserable wooden shanties, which have sprung into existence since the war began. For an immense distance endless bales of cotton are to be seen."[14] On September 6, 1864, however, fortunes changed when the French at Bagdad defeated Cortina and his men, who were probably *Aguilas*. They quickly crossed the Rio Grande and were temporarily interned by the Union Army, but they were released a few days later and aided the United States federal forces.[15]

Throughout the 1860s, the *Aguilas* had a special recruiting office in Brownsville to raise troops to fight the French forces in

Mexico. Some of the staff may even have been part of the Union army. Ernst Pitner, one of Maximilian's lieutenants, probably referred to them when he wrote about the headquarters of dissident leaders: "From there they are provided with men, with money, with water and munitions, and also with intelligence. They wander around everywhere openly and ostentatiously, fraternize with the Yankees, regularly insult all those of imperial sympathies and people going there from Matamoros-in short, they behave more or less as if they were the lords of creation and threaten twenty times a day to make a meal of us here."[16]

The *Aguilas* also spied for others, providing that Juan Cortina approved. As a courtesy, Cortina helped Union Army General Phillip Sheridan, who apparently sent four of his most trusty men "to glean information regarding the movements of the Imperial forces and also to gather intelligence about the ex-Confederates who had crossed the Rio Grande."[17] Sheridan was interested in "certain munitions of war that had been turned over by ex-Confederates to the Imperial General [Mejia] commanding at Matamoros."[18] As Canales commented, "Sheridan's men needed aides that knew the region, the culture, language, and key political figures along the Rio Grande. In support of the Union and Juarez, the *Aguilas* were used."[19] But *Aguila* support for Sheridan ended when the political winds changed and Sheridan personally became involved in Mexican politics opposing Cortina.

Police and Raiders

Jose Canales believed that the *Aguilas* served the function of police and security force in that they kept track of renegades, traitors, rascals, idealists, merciless fortune seekers, erroneous patriots, misguided martyrs, mysterious bureaucrats, deceptive and keen enemies. An old friend of Richard King, a frail, soft-spoken lawman, Leander H. McNelly, referred to some of Cortina's forces as the Matamoros "mounted police force" which served as Cortina's personal guard.[20] He explained that they were "used . . . to arrest criminals and to preserve the peace generally, but more especially to guard against invasions or incursions."[21]

McNelly may have been describing the *Exploradores* and the *Aguilas* when he referred to them as Mexican bandits "patrolling the bank of the river up and down . . . very watchful and efficient." They had a "perfect and efficient system of guards and patrols, which [made] it impossible for any party to enter their country without being noticed, and confronted in a short time by a considerable force."[22] McNelly also took note of their courier activities as they carried messages "very rapidly . . . at least fifteen miles an hour."[23]

The *Aguilas* had a committee for the protection of social order. After carefully deliberating the nature of the crime and finding an individual guilty, it was determined how the criminal should be punished. The execution of the sentence took place at once in order to prevent a rescue by other criminals or friends. Usually he was whipped or hanged, which led Canales to conclude that the "committee of Aguilas acted as judge, jury and executioner."[24] Such vigorous methods of justice were also evident in California, Idaho, and Montana. In New Mexico, there were vigilante actions by groups such as the *Mano Negra* and the *Gorras Blancas*. Similar to the *Aguilas*, the *Gorras Blancas* remained a terrorist, secretive group, thereby making it very difficult to identify and bring charges against participants of guerrilla raids. They were always on the offensive, sabotaging the efforts of Anglo American land grabbers.

In reality the *Aguilas* had to provide and enforce the law since the legal system along the lower Rio Grande was corrupt and racist. Their methods were perceived by their supporters as more efficient than the complex system of courts, juries, attorneys and jails in that violent, turbulent society. The *Aguilas* existed as a response to lawlessness and unpopular laws that created fear in bewildered people.[25] As Paul S. Taylor wrote: "The lives of Mexicans, like their property, were insecure and unequally protected." In 1878, for example, the American consul at Matamoros wrote, "when it is known that a Mexican has been hung or killed in the neighborhood of Brownsville, or along the frontier, there is seldom any fuss made about it."[26] Taylor explained that, ". . . confusion, robbery, arson, and bloodshed were common in south Texas in the middle seventies . . . emotions . . . were crystallized along race lines,"[27] leading Canales to remark: "The soul of the age was cruelty, and the heart of justice a stone."[28]

The *Aguilas* resisted fighting major battles with American law enforcement and usually resorted to hit-and-run tactics. One officer writing to General Sherman in 1875, described the situation this way:

> *The country between Corpus Christi and the Rio Grande is in a state of confusion and war, and is full of armed bandits and Mexicans, robbing and devastating the whole section. Five ranches have been burned, and several people killed and wounded. Wires cut between Corpus Christi and Brownsville. A courier sent from King's Ranch brings intelligence that they are surrounded by a large party of Mexicans, and ask for aid.*"[29]

The *Aguilas* were also very effective in demoralizing their enemies. They launched their lightening raids at night when the enemy was asleep. They calculated that the surprised enemy required five minutes to be suitable for combat after being awakened. Their motive was to battle fast and furiously and then withdraw quickly. Moreover, these raids were meticulously planned so that the *Aguilas*, in their black robes, could quickly disappear into the night. These tactics were so effective that Texas Governor Richard Coke wrote in April 1875: "The alarm in this country . . . upon these raids, in which our people are ruthlessly murdered and their property forcibly taken . . . is widespread, and unless relieved . . . must result in a general breakup of the settlements."[30]

They also enjoyed tremendous local support. In return for local hospitality, the *Aguilas* divided the gratuity from their raids, which included cattle, foodstuffs and other supplies with local farmers and other people who had done them favors.[31] They had strict rules toward those who offered them shelter. For example, no one took a thing without permission, and those who violated such rules were quickly sent to the regular army of *Fieles*.[32] The *Aguilas* wanted only dedicated fighters and weeded out any one who was incompetent.

Spies and Scouts

The *Aguilas* oversaw an intricate network of espionage that furthered the political and social objectives of Cortina. They commanded hundred of agents, informers, and a counter intelligence group.[33] McNelly Ranger, Captain Neal Coldwell was probably referring to the "*Aguilas*" when he stated:

These bandit groups are too smart and too well organized. They've got spies everywhere. They know where every soldier and every Ranger outfit is, and they know your moves before you can make them. They're bigger and smarter than the law.[34]

Another McNelly Ranger, George Durham, expressed his admiration for Cortina's spy system:

The Cortinistas had a big edge. They had two hundred miles of river they could dart across, then get lost in the back country till they put together a herd. They had a good spy system and appeared to know where every soldier or Ranger was at any time, day or night. And they had hundreds and hundreds of men. Captain [L.H. McNelly] had twenty-nine.[35]

Yet another 1875 reference, perhaps describing the *Aguilas*, referred to "a large floating population who have no permanent abode anywhere, and who are the spies and informers of the raiders."[36] These agents "worked so systemically and were so perfectly organized that they successfully defied or eluded all attempts to bring them to justice. They laughed at the abortive attempts of the United States cavalry to catch them . . . and could always escape across the Rio Grande."[37]

Evidence exists that in order to safeguard the secrecy of their organization, the Cortinistas declared all out war against corruption within as well as outside their own ranks. They terrorized suspected traitors and informers: "At night, dressed in flowing black gowns with long hoods, the *Aguilas* would surprise the suspected traitors and warn them of further consequences if certain actions were not stopped."[38] General Edward O.C. Ord observed on February 12th, 1876, that the *Cortinistas* "have always taken precautions to cover their movements, and to keep the information of their raids from spreading. Where they discovered that information had been given of their movements, they murdered the man who sent it and the boy who took it."[39]

It is clear that the *Aguilas*' methods were extremely effective. For example, adjutant General William Steele wrote in 1875: "The thieves and cutthroat. . . think the killing of a Texan something to be proud of . . . even of their own nationality . . . Many have been killed for no other reason than that they knew too much."[40] *Aguilas*' methods, though brutal, bore fruit. Steele confessed: "The result is that they [Mexicans] . . . will not willingly give information."[41] Colonel J. H. Potter, investigating a disappearance, wrote: "The class of people that do know all about the matter will not inform, for fear that they may disappear also; at least they say so. There have been several murders within a year."[42]

Carlos Esparza, who headed a group of *Aguilas,* appeared to many as an ordinary rancher, possessing neither Cortina's striking appearance nor obvious leadership qualities.[43] He proved to be, however, a canny leader and shaped the *Aguilas* into an efficient instrument for the Cortinista interests. Cortina gave him an honorary superintendent's position in Matamoros so that he would have access to city resources to benefit the *Aguilas*.[44] Of Carlos Esparza, Jose

Canales commented: "It must have been the will of God for Esparza not to be hanged or shot, since most of the *Aguilas'* activities were engineered by him. I guess his talents saved him. He continued to be an enigmatic man, supervising thriving [a] network of spies."[45]

According to Canales, the *Aguilas* had what amounted to a training manual on psychological and guerrilla warfare, and Canales believed Esparza himself authored it. It detailed a variety of persuasion techniques ranging from helping farmers harvest their crops to assassinations. It explained how to 'neutralize' public officials, such as judges, sheriffs, and law enforcement officials. Manual rules required citizens to be assembled to witness the execution of a traitor, who was presented as "an enemy of the people."[46]

A zealous *Aguila*, Ramon Garcia, was the father-in-law of Carlos Esparza. This perceptive, tenacious and plain, no-frills farmer, always wore a large broad-brimmed hat, and managed to build a thriving business selling firewood and dry goods to the river boats and farmers. On May 24, 1862, he was issued a Confederate pass to sell Confederate bonds to the Hispanic community up and down the lower Rio Grande. Ironically, he sold them in return for Mexican silver pesos since the Confederate currency itself had little value.[47]

Garcia was admired by John Ford, Santos Benavides and other zealous Confederates. But what they failed to understand was that Garcia's bond sales were nothing but a masquerade to spy on Cortina's enemies. These bonds were always purchased by Carlos Esparza or another *Aguila* and were used skillfully by Garcia to communicate with Esparza through code. If Esparza obtained a Jefferson Davis $10 bond it meant that Ford was getting ready to battle the *Cortinistas*. If Esparza acquired a different Confederate patriotic $50 bond, it meant Cortina should stay in Matamoros because the *Cortinista* enemies were patrolling the lower Rio Grande. If he collected a "Stonewall Jackson" $10 bond it meant that all was well. This scheme became more complicated as the Civil War endured.

Juan N. Cortina

The *Aguilas Negras* enforced a rough frontier justice, one that reflected the *Tejano* frustration with the American conquest. At the same time this para-military group was an example of how Cortina's organizations genuinely enabled *Tejanos* to maintain control of the lower Rio Grande well into the 1870s.

1. Canales interview, August 12, 1964. For more on the Cortina era, see Jerry Thompson, ed., Fifty Miles and a Fight: Major Samuel Peter Heintzelman's Journal of Texas and the Cortina War (Austin: Texas State Historical Association, 1998), 23-191.

2. Rodolfo Acuña to the author (Larralde), February 9, 1979; Arnoldo De Leon to the author, March 29,1989. Acuña noted: "I am (also) dropping references to *Los Fieles* and *Los Exploradores* since I cannot find any basis of fact for them." However, the Reports of Mexican Border Commission mentions them, except for the *Aguilas*. Acuña denied that there were *Aguilas* since Cortina did not have spies. Yet he wrote, "On the U.S. side, a network of supporters, who acted as spies, aided Cortina" in his Occupied America: A History of Chicanos (New York: Harper Collins, 1988), 46. The question again arises, who were Cortina's spies and how did they function?

3. Canales Interview, August 12,1964. Also, Philip S. Foner, A History of Cuba and Its Relations with the United States (New York: International Publishers, 1962), 1:122.

4. There were other organizations with similar traits such as the *Aguilas Negras* in New Mexico. The *Gorras Blancas* (White Caps) were active from 1889-1891 in northern New Mexico. They were "a band of night riders... wearing masks to avoid detection... to cut down fences and burn barns and haystacks," wrote Robert W. Larson, Populism in the Mountain West (Albuquerque: University of New Mexico, 1986), 113.

    The historian Robert Rosenbaum provides the most extensive research on *Las* Gonas *Negras*. They were active in Colfax County, New Mexico. The leader was Eugenio Romero who "was in the county trying to organize a chapter of the Law and Order Society." Robert J. Rosenbaum, Mexicano Resistance in the Southwest: "The Sacred Right of Self-Preservation" (Austin: University of Texas Press, 1981), 212.

    La Mano Negra (The Black Hand) functioned in northwestern New Mexico as late as the 1920s. As for details, this organization is in need of historical research. See Nancie L. Gonzalez, The Spanish-American of New Mexico: A Heritage of Pride (Albuquerque: University of New Mexico, 1967), 90,180.

5. Canales Interview, August 12,1964.

6. Torrea, Estado de Tamaulipas, 112; Canales Interview, November 16, 1964; A. Brooke Caruso The Mexican Spy Company: United States Covert Operations in Mexico, 1845-1848 (Jefferson, North Carolina: McFarland & Company,1991), 85. "Again, the

5.   Canales Interview, August 12,1964.

6.   Torrea, Estado de Tamaulipas, 112; Canales Interview, November 16, 1964; A. Brooke Caruso The Mexican Spy Company: United States Covert Operations in Mexico, 1845-1848 (Jefferson, North Carolina: McFarland & Company,1991), 85. "Again, the language barrier made effective covert intelligence collection operations difficult. Mexicans who supplied information to the Americans could have been bearers of disinformation or collectors of information for the Mexican military."

7.   John James Peck, The Sign of the Eagle (San Diego *Union Tribune*, 1970), 18.

8.   Cortina realized the value of what a spy system could do for a cause. See Kearney and Knopp, Boom and Bust 59, 162.

9.   Samuel C. Reid, The Scouting Expeditions of McCulloch's Texas Rangers (Philadelphia: John E. Potter and Co., 1875), 114

10. Rayburn and Rayburn, Centuries of Conflict, 69.

11. Canales Interview, November 16,1964.

12. Canales Interview, November 18, 1964. Pitner, 102.

13. Canales did not know the date. He also was not certain of the full name of Milan. See Richard T. Marcum, "Fort Brown, Texas: The History of a Border Post," Ph.D. dissertation, Texas Technological College, 1964, 167-168; Kearney and Knopp, Boom and Bust, 132.
     Canales said that Milan was known as *El Picodo,* who had a talent for organization. He was unpopular since he insisted on rigid discipline among the *Aguilas* and among other *Cortinistas.*

14. Fremantle, Diary, 3.

15. Pitner, 101

16. Ibid.,108.

17. Sheridan, Memoirs, 2: 214. Some Confederate exiles such as Confederate General Jubal Early were warned that it was too dangerous to cross the Rio Grande into Mexico. "The route over the Rio Grande has become impracticable on accounts of robbers and guerrillas." These "guerrillas" may have been the *Cortinistas,* especially the *Aguilas Negras.*

So dangerous was the Rio Grande that Early decided to take the sea route to Veracruz where he arrived onDecember 27,1865. Mexico offered almost nothing

Juan N. Cortina

19. Canales Interview, November 16,1964.

20. See Testimony of S.H. McNally (sic), January 24,1876, in U. S. Congress, House Report, 44th Congress, 1st Session, number 34, "Texas Frontier Troubles," Vol. 1876-1877, Serial Number 1709, Washington: Government Printing Office, 1877, 11, 12, (Hereafter cited as "Texas Frontier Troubles". "McNelly" is sometimes variantly spelled "McNally." For a recent evaluation on Leander McNelly see Robert Draper, "The Twilight of the Texas Rangers, Texas Monthly, February 1994, 80.

21. Ibid.

22. Ibid., xii.

23. Ibid., 11-12.

24. Canales Interview, November 12, 1964. The Aguilas and the San Francisco Committee of Vigilance had similar concepts of justice. See Williams, David C. Broderick, 62.

25. Canales Interview, November 12, 1964.

26. Paul Schuster Taylor, An American-Mexican Frontier: Nueces County, Texas (Chapel Hill: University of North Carolina, 1934), 65.

27. Ibid., 66.

28. Canales Interview, November 12,1964.

29. Quoted in W.T. Sherman to W. W. Belknap, April 20, 1875 in "Texas Frontier Troubles," 73.

30. Richard Coke to General E.O.C. Ord, April 24,1875 in ibid., 71. See also the Austin Statesman, June 16, 27, 1874, depicting Mexicans killing Anglos and Anglos killing Mexicans.

31. Ibid., 156-157. This source did not refer to them as Aguilas. Canales discovered this later during his oral interviews.

32. Canales Interview, November 12, 1964. Apparently activities of the Aguilas were nothing exceptional during this era. During the American Civil War, John Singleton Mosby and his men did the same thing. The Civil War: Spies, Scouts and Raiders, Irregular Operations (Alexandria: Time-Life, 1985), 127-128.

33. Canales Interview, August 12,1964. NA. Jennings, Texas Rangers, 160-161, wrote about such informers: "We prepared to go to meet them and give them a warm reception; but before we started, a scout came in and told us that the leader of the gang had been assassinated by one of his own men... the raid had been abandoned."

Canales said that the leader, Sapo Garcia, was shot for treason by the *Aguilas*. The Mexican who handed a note to Lieutenant Robertson was an *Aguila* spy who discovered Sapo's treason.

34.   George Durham Taming the Nueces Strip: The Story of Mcnelly's Rangers (Austin: University of Texas Press, 1962), 41-42.

       Bern Keating, An Illustrated History of the Texas Rang ers (New York: Rand McNally & Co., 1975), 107 wrote that Durham stayed with the special border force beyond McNelly's death from tuberculosis. He ended his days as a foreman on the huge King Ranch.

35.   Durham, Taming the Nueces Strip, 87.

36.   "Texas Frontier Troubles," xiii.

37.   Jennings, Texas Rangers, 108.

38.   Canales Interview, August 12, 1964. For the same reasons, the Rangers also did most of their activities at night. As Jennings, Texas Rangers, 147, said: "This was for two reasons; our movements at night did not attract so much attention, and then, in that hot climate, night-riding is less severe on horses than travelling under the blazing semi-tropical sun."

39.   Testimony of General E.O.C. Ord, February 12,1876, "Texas Frontier Troubles," 33. The San Antonio *Express*, February 16, 1876, reported that Ord testified before the Mexican Border Committee. (testimony reprinted in House Report No.343, 44 Cong., I Sess., Ser. 1709). See also Austin *Statesman*, June 16, 17, 1874, depicting atrocities along the lower Rio Grande.

40.   W.M. Steele to the Adjutant General, July 1, 1875, "Texas Frontier Troubles," 122.

41.   Ibid.

42.   J.H. Potter to the Adjutant General, May 12, 1875, in ibid., 113.

43.   Canales Interview, August 12,1964. Canales was captivated with Carlos Esparza. I too became engrossed with the man, partly because he was the grandfather of my grandmother, Francisca Esparza Montalvo. In a way he was also part of my youth. Most of the furniture in my home originally was his. I also inherited his personal papers which included legal documents and letters. One contains a strange code that may reflect his spying or business activities.
In the 1970s, I was completing my doctoral dissertation at UCLA. I went to what is now the Barker Texas History Center at the University of Texas at Austin. While examining the Jose San Roman Papers, I discovered several papers with the same code. Such a discovery was not surprising since San Roman was a business associate of Esparza.

They both needed each other to survive in a turbulent region. As for the papers, they were crumbling from age and were not on microfilm.

44.   Ibid.

45.   Canales Interview, June 10,1964. During the 1860s another man similar to Esparza had the same style and talent as a spy. He was the Confederate Thomas Nelson Conrad who was active in the Washington D.C. area. Also during our current era, Markus Wolf ran "Communist East Germany's devastatingly successful network of Cold War spies." Wolf himself was known as the "man without a face" due to "his canny ability to avoid being photographed," wrote Tamara Jones, "Former Chief of E. German Spy Ring Charged," Los Angeles *Times,* September 25, 1992.

46.   Ibid.

47.   I have the Ramon Garcia Papers, which include the original Confederate permit document, May 24,1862, as well as several other letters. The Garcia Papers also contain numerous Confederate bonds. These items refer to bonds or other issues in Louisiana, Texas, and Arkansas. Special stamps were prepared for Houston and Marshall, Texas, to prevent bonds sent from Richmond to that region from being captured and used by the Union.

My grandmother, Francisca Esparza Montalvo, knew about Ramon Garcia. He was her great-grandfather and she heard of his exploits through her grandmother, Francisca Garcia Esparza, the wife of Carlos Esparza. In time, my grandmother gave Canales the Ramon Garcia Papers for his historical studies. He eventually gave them to me.

The information on Ramon Garcia was related to me by my grandmother during the summer of 1959. Canales visited her to reflect on her family's recollections. Canales had a soothing way of getting people to talk about their family, even if they were strangers to him. It was a skill that he developed out of necessity when he needed to gather court evidence for his cases.

CHAPTER IX

Terror and Repression

The *Aguilas Negras* developed a frightful reputation for their actions which in turn earned them unparalleled persecution, torture, and death if captured. In fact, it is safe to state that the *Aguilas* degree of success was matched only by the degree of violence they faced if captured.

The *Aguilas'* courage was well recognized and feared even by those who hunted them. Leander.H. McNelly who fought the *Aguilas Negras*, stated, "I have never seen men fight with such desperation. Many of them after being shot from their horses and severely wounded three or four times would rise on their elbows and fire on my men as they passed."[1] One of McNelly's men, George Durham, said of Cortina's men, "They were forded and sheltered and ready for engagement. They fought desperately, every one firing his pistol so long as he could raise up, even when mortally wounded."[2] Another lawman, N. A. Jennings commented: "Some of our enemies were well mounted . . . Some of them fought so desperately that even when dismounted and wounded four or five times they continued to shoot at us."[3]

This recognition of *Aguilas* courage in no way translated to any form of respect or humane treatment if captured. As was the case with any of Cortina's men, if an *Aguilas Negra* was captured he faced torture and death. According to Lawman William Callicot, McNelly hired a sadistic Mexican named Jesus Sandoval to torture and hang every captured Cortinista.[4] McNelly, described by W. P. Webb, historian of the Rangers, "as a tallish man of quiet manner, and with the soft voice of a timid Methodist preacher," who kept no prisoners.[5]

111

Callicot stated, "If we turned a spy loose he would spread the news among the bandits and we would never catch them."[6] Thus, according to Canales, "McNelly's Mexican prisoners were brutally tortured and murdered. Then they were buried in unmarked graves to hide the atrocities."[7] He added that, "McNelly's troops were the engine of terror or the Gestapo of Texas. It grew firmer and more formidable." "It was also an engine of fanaticism, an instrument of repression and murder. McNelly carried a Bible to rationalize his extermination of those who he saw not fit to live."[8]

Ironically, it was through his Bible readings, that McNelly regarded most Mexicans as a race permanently warped by a hereditary flaw. To him, numerous torture devices were valid to get *Cortinistas* to talk or betray their fellow soldiers, including cutting off their ears, fingers, toes or worse, skinning them alive. Even *gringos* who were fighting for Cortina suffered the same fate. General Ord stated, "Captain McNelly had a big advantage over the United States troops mainly because he employed means of getting information from prisoners that was denied the military. His prisoners would talk. Ours wouldn't."[9] A determined Jesus Sandoval helped McNelly decimate every *Aguila* he could find. According to Dora Neil Raymond, "He had a personal vendetta which accounted for his hatred of his race and for the assaults that won him a name as the scourge of the border." [10] Raymond further notes:

> *When McNelly instituted his spy system, Sandoval helped by cruelly unique methods of gaining information from the spies of his opponents. The Captain preferred not to witness all of the activities of Jesús, nor to ask what became of Mexican scouts when they had been drained of their secrets. Officers of the Regular Army, were debarred from using such men as Sandoval.[11]*

Ranger William Callicott, himself, told Walter Prescott Webb about the procedures used by "Old Casuse," Sandoval's nick name.

"Two or three men marched on each side of the company in the direction we were going and looked out for bandits and spies, and if they came across a Mexican that looked suspicious they would bring him to the company for "Old Casuse" to identify."[12] If the captive was suspected as an *Aguila*, his life was in jeopardy. "If he proved to be a bandit spy one of us would take charge of him and march along until we saw a suitable tree." There the Rangers would put the rope over the captive's neck "and torture him by cutting him slowly to expose and pull out his intestines or by skinning him alive."[13]

According to Canales, "Casuse was fond of escorting these Mexicans to execution, always scrutinizing the expressions of horror on their faces. He enjoyed seeing their faces distorted by terror, especially when they were howling in pain."[14] Some of the disfigured bodies that smelled terribly were transported to Brownsville as war trophies. One report stated, "They brought back . . . eight bodies of dead Mexicans--all that could be found--and placed them on the public square."[15] Two historians, J. Lee Stambaugh and Lillian J. Stambaugh have attempted to justify such cruelty: "These spies were executed by hanging, because the Rangers did not have sufficient men and food to care for the prisoners, and to release them would have defeated the purpose of the campaign."[16]

Indeed, despite the atrocities commited, some historians have even gone so far as to glorify McNelly. Rupert Norval Richardson wrote, "In courage and audacity the record of McNelly's force has never been surpassed."[17] Writer T. R. Fehrenbach stated, "McNelly was a great captain. He was the epitome of the Texan in action, and he set a record of courage, cunning, and audacity that was never to be surpassed."[18] Another author, Bern Keating painted a less romantic picture of McNelly. He noted, "A ruthless campaigner, Captain McNelly was probably the last of the old guerrilla warriors who made up the law as they went along, dealing out justice, as they saw it, on the spot. He excited almost fanatic loyalty among his men."[19]

Journalist Robert Draper wrote of McNelly "To the Rangers and their admiring historians, McNelly is an appealing composite of warlord and Christ figure: courageous and gentlemanly, utterly devoted to his men and his mission, a remorseless killer, and dead himself by the holy age of 33." He added, "From McNelly flows the rich blood of Ranger lore. And that is oddly fitting, since in fact Leander McNelly was never a Texas Ranger."[20] Rodolfo Acuña adds that, "McNelly tortured Mexicans and shot them down in cold blood. On November 19, 1875, he crossed the border with 31 men and attacked a ranch that he thought housed Mexican troops. He was mistaken, and he murdered a number of innocent Mexican workers. When he discovered his error, he merely rode off."[21]

Those "Little McNellys"

The tough band of Rangers who followed McNelly were dedicated to his principles "with a devotion bordering on fanaticism."[22] They were proud to call themselves "Little McNellys," especially those under Captain J. L. Hall and Lieutenant John B. Armstrong. As Walter Prescott Webb said of McNelly, "No better man, probably, could have been found for this assignment. He was a frail man, then dying of tuberculosis, but he managed to live a little more than two years, and to make a record unmatched among Texas Rangers of all time."[23] While suffering from this chronic disease and resting on a wagon bed, McNelly instructed his men to enforce his concept of justice. He never had to worry. Sometimes he steered them throughout the day without saying a word. To these men, human life and dignity lost all meaning because they had the power of life and death over the Mexicans along the lower Rio Grande, they could shoot to kill. Mexicans had no rights or authority of any kind, and they could be searched and their property seized at a moment's notice.

McNelly faithfully read the Bible for moral guidance, never knowing what mercy and understanding meant and he remained uncannily cold and aloof with the Mexican public. His effectiveness came from his troops whose loyalty was cultivated and guaranteed by his placing them above the law. In so doing, he gave them a sense of boldness and fortitude over their insecure and unstable lives; nothing else mattered. Consequently, these men created their own conditions for shooting and hanging anyone who stood in their way, leaving corpses stiffening in the contorted agony of death. According to T. R. Fehrenbach, "the Rangers were considered a military force, not policemen."[24] McNelly's Rangers, in the words of Canales, "were certainly killers and thieves themselves" and they were anxious to have these Mexicans defeated, disillusioned, and demoralized.[25] In turn, the *Cortinistas*, especially the *Aguilas*, were determined to eliminate the Texas Rangers.

Ranger Armstrong followed in McNelly's footsteps. Webb wrote of him, "One does not have to follow John Armstrong's career very far to recognize that he was a man after McNelly's own heart. His methods were McNelly's methods and he never hesitated to administer extreme unction to those who could not be handled in a more gentle manner. The episodes for which he was solely responsible are so stirring that they deserve separate notice."[26] There is no doubt that Armstrong was involved in countless episodes of mass murder even though they remain poorly documented. According to Canales, the passage of time has erased most of the evidence. No one dared to verify eyewitness accounts into written or printed pages. It simply was too dangerous to criticize the Rangers for their tortured victims, especially of innocent women and children.

Hanging bodies were a common sight, particularly those of the *Aguilas*. The trees were used for these executions, mainly along the Military Road from Brownsville to Santa Maria and further up the river. According to Canales "There were mutilated, fast-decaying corpses. The hair and the skin drooped from the head. The flesh crumpled from the bones with repulsive maggots in it. People who passed by had to stuff their nostrils with rags." The stench was nauseating. The blistering heat of the summer made it more unbearable while swarms of flies hovered over these decaying corpses. "As a child, I remembered people finding skulls and bones in remote parts of the countryside that belonged to some of these victims."[27] Much of this is not known. The legacy of the "Little McNellys" has rarely been examined in perspective. Those accounts which have been written are far less than accurate. For example, one account states "The reputation of these men has endured as of a ghastly aberration to be silenced or stifled up as rapidly as possible. This chronicle has been sutured off from the annals of Texas history."[28]

Despite the wave of terror, resistance remained strong in the Mexican community. When Captain Ford hired Mexicans as spies, the *Aguilas* hired double agents.[29] In his edition of John Ford's recollections, Stephen Oates writes:

> *An old gentlemen of Reynosa . . . one of Ford's old friends . . . . agreed to furnish information on the numbers and intentions of the Mexican forces. . . acting as a spy. The real object of his old friend's coming was to find out all he could about the ranger force.*[30]

The *Aguilas* had partisans and agents everywhere. "They could have been priests, soldiers, vendors of sweets and cakes, beggars, or winesellers. They could have been women performing domestic duties, picking up information here and there while getting water, shopping for food, or beating clothes against stone slabs."[31] Bits of news obtained were funneled through secret channels for investigation by the *Aguilas*. In 1875, Samuel J. Stewart narrated, "The Mexicans on this side of the Rio Grande are not willing to give information or assist the officers to make arrests; but, on the contrary, they give aid and comfort to the bands of thieves and murderers from Mexico."[32] The "Aguilas existed like a many limbed serpent, moving slowly in and out, back and forth, cutting back here, growing new limbs there, renewing its strength and keeping surveillance . . . protected by a citizenry which knew nothing."[33] Through these tactics, the silent *Aguilas* in their black gowns in the night searched for Jesus Sandoval.[34] "For several months," Sandoval wrote, "I have not slept in my house; I have slept in the chaparral--and have been a solitary sentinel over my own person."[35] The dreaded months extended to miserable years of solitude until his health was amost totally destroyed.

Despite the fanatical efforts of the Rangers, most of the *Aguilas* managed to survive while Juan Cortina remained out of reach. Not only did they survive but they remained active until about 1880. "They were well disciplined and self-sufficient and they managed to function without a major leader."[36] This was vital once Cortina moved to Mexico City. In part, due to the *Aguilas*, Juan Cortina maintained a solid power base in the lower Rio Grande Valley. According to Canales, "men like Carlos Esparza made certain that Cortina's authority always remained intact."[37]

Deplorable conditions well after the Mexican War made it inevitable that a populist spokesman, leader, and civil rights advocate would find impassioned support. Cortina was one of these leaders. According to Canales, "Wherever he [Cortina] went, he gave hope for a better life to desperate people who were seeking justice." [38] In 1877, Gen. William T. Sherman testified: "Cortina is simply a creation. If you kill Cortina, another like creation will come in his place."[39]

1. Quoted in Webb, Texas Rangers, 240. For more on Aguja see Jennings, A Texas Ranger, 139. Jennings relates how the leader of the raiders, Espinosa, was killed by McNelly during a gun fight.
    Canales said Espinosa was one of Cortina's more capable commanders of guerrillas before his untimely death. Nacho Espinosa was a cavalry officer who did much to boost morale. He reorganized his mounted troopers into a fierce battalion that served Cortina in offensive and defensive operations.

2. Durham, Taming the Nueces Strip, 57.

3. Jennings, A Texas Ranger, 137.

4. For other atrocities by McNelly's Rangers, see Mexico City *Diaro Oficial*, November 23, 25, 1875, Matamoros *Voz del Pueblo*, November 10-25, 1875. Also Notes from the Mexican Legation in the United States to the Department of State, Record Group 59, Roll 106, National Archives, Washington, D.C.

Jennings, A Texas Ranger, 1411-47, illustrate how McNelly's men would torment Mexicans during festivities by shooting out the lights. "This would naturally result in much confusion and, added to the reports of our revolvers, would be the shrill screaming of women and the cursing of angry Mexicans."

5.   Quoted in Rupert Norval Richardson, Texas; The Lone Star State (Englewood Cliffs: Prentice-Hall, 1956), 306.

6.   See also Jennings, A Texas Ranger, 148-158 for Frank Sandoval. Sandoval may have murdered forty or fifty men and burned scores of ranches due to his hate for fellow Mexicans. "I have good reason to be convinced that Captain McNelly knew positively Sandoval was the dreaded border scourge, and I suspect that it was for that very reason he enlisted him in the troop," Jennings recalled.

7.   Canales Interview, November 16, 1964.

8.   Ibid.

McNelly's and his "Little McNelly's" extermination program was not unusual. During this period, Gen. William T. Sherman told an audience in Connecticut that the extermination of the Pequots in 1637 had been right because it had made possible the Connecticut of 1881.
During the Civil War, Sherman saw his victims as "weak or deluded or obsolete and therefore about to be crushed." In August 1862, he wrote, "We must begin at Kentucky and reconquer the country from them as we did from the Indians. It was this conviction then as plainly as now that made men think I was insane."
To Sherman, Indian resistance seemed little more than an irritant. "The conflict grew portentous in his rhetorc when he was using defeat of the Indians to confirm his faith, which he never freed from doubt, that the United States must be the nation of the future. Sanity lay in success." See Charles Royster The Destructive War: William Tecumseh Sherman, Stonewall Jackson, and the Americans (New York: Alfred A. Knopf, 1991), 396-398.

9.   Quoted in Durham, Taming the Nueces Strip, 55. Canales interview, November 16, 1964. Unlike Federal troops, McNelly raided Mexico to promote his concept of justice. See the San Antonio *Express*, December 2, 1875; the Matamoros *Heraldo del Bravo*, December 1, 2, 1875.

10.   Dora Neill Raymond, Captain Lee Hall of Texas (Norman: University of Oklahoma Press, 1940), 51.

11.   Ibid.

12.   Webb, Texas Rangers, 243.

13.   Canales Interview, November 16,1964.

14.   Ibid.

15.   Canales Interview, November 16, 1964. Also, Stambaugh, Lower Rio Grande Valley, 152-53; Keating, An Illustrated History, 113-114.

16.   Stambaugh, Lower Rio Grande Valley, 152.

17.   Richardson, Texas, 306.

18.   Fehrenbach, Lone Star, 575.

19.   Keating, An Illustrated History, 106.

20.   Robert Draper, "The Twilight of the Texas Rangers," Texas Monthly, February, 1994, 80, 82.

21.   Acuña, Occupied America, 40.

22.   Lamar, Resder's Encyclopedia, 701.

       A majority of scholars who studied the *Cortinistas* and the Texas Rangers ignored the fact that the Rangers and most United States soldiers were equipped with the marvelous Winchester rifles. By 1862, the rifle could "be discharged 16 times without loading or taking down from the shoulder, or even loosing aim. . . it can be instantly used without taking the strap from the shoulder."
       Even the "Little McNelly's" fanaticism was enforced with the light, effective Winchester rifles and Colt single-action pistols. Also the American Indians cherished them. Chief Poundmaker of the Crees was once photographed with his Model 1866 rifle. It had a sling attached. Mexican President Porfirio Diaz had a "Model 1866" with "a Mexican eagle carved in relief on the ivory stock." So rare is the Diaz carbine that it is known to collectors as the ivory-stocked Winchester. See: R.L. Wilson, Winchester. An American Legend:The Official History of Winchester Firearms and Ammunition from 1849 to the Present (New York: Random House, 1991), 18, 27, 29,100.

23.   Quoted in Durham, Taming the Nueces Strip, ix.

24.   Fehrenbach, Lone Star, 576.

25.   Canales Interview, November 16, 1964. See also Draper, 82.

26.   Webb, Texas Rangers, 294-295.

27.   Canales Interview, November 16, 1964. Some of these atrocities were reported by the San Antonio *Express*, June 14,19, 21,1875. Primarily on June 19, the newspaper stated

27. Canales Interview, November 16, 1964. Some of these atrocities were reported by the San Antonio *Express*, June 14,19, 21,1875. Primarily on June 19, the newspaper stated that McNelly murdered "thirteen Mexicans last week. Another Mexican killed near the Medina." The issue of June 21, stated that Mexicans were discovered dead on the public highways and that Governor Richard Coke attempted to resolve the border troubles by killing more Mexicans.

28. Ibid.

29. Canales Interview, June 10,1964; see Ford, Rip Ford's Texas, 298 for "Mexicans employed as spies." Jennings wrote that George Hall spied on Cortina. Such an assertion is questionable. Jennings, A Texas Ranger, 140.

30. Ford, Rip Ford's Texas, 302-303.

31. Canales Interview, June 10, 1964.

32. Samuel J. Stewart to General E.O.C. Ord, June 8,1875, "Texas Frontier Troubles," 114. Also, San Antonio *Daily Express,* August 25, 1877; extract from a Mier newspaper *(El Azote),* cited by Webb, The Texas Rangers, 294.

33. Canales Interview, August 12,1964.

34. Ibid.

35. Quoted in Raymond, Captain Lee Hall, 51. Sandoval filed an affidavit on May 3, 1875 recalling his life "as a traitor to Mexico."

36. Canales Interview, August 12, 1964.

37. Ibid.

38. Canales Interview, August 12,1964. By 1877 Texas wanted to send U.S. troops into Mexico to crush every Chicano rebel. See excerpts from the Belton *Journal,* Castroville *Era,* Houston *Telegram,* Cuero *Bulletin,* and Houston *Age* in the San Antonio *Daily Express*, September 21,1877; other excerpts from the Austin *Gazette*, Houston *Telegram,* Corpus Christ *Gazette*, and Houston *Age* in ibid., September 23, 1877.

39. Testimony of William T. Sherman, 1877, U.S. Congress, House Report, 45th Cong., 2nd Sess., Serial No. 1820, "Testimony taken by the Committee on Military Affairs in relation to The Texas Border Troubles" (Washington, D.C.: Government Printing Office, 1878), 35.

CHAPTER X

Las Mujeres Cortinistas

Women played an extremely important role in the *Cortinista's* struggle for justice and liberation in south Texas just as they would in the Mexican Revolution of 1910. It was Canales who discovered numerous women, later termed *Aguilas Damas*. They fought and spied for Cortina's army during and after the American Civil War, and in the early 1900s, Canales interviewed several of them. Beyond the few names and stories obtained through Canales' research, however, we can only speculate as to the actual number, activities, motivations, and accomplishments of the Cortinista women.

From the interviews conducted by Canales, we may deduce that most of these women had either witnessed or been subjected to violence, including rape. Some had been forced into prostituion in order to survive. Rather than continue as passive victims, they chose to act by serving the *Cortinista* cause in the capacity of spies, smugglers, cooks, nurses, or messengers. Many even served as soldiers. Known as *soldaderas,* some of these courageous women dressed as men and engaged in battle, several of them dying in the conflict. Women also carried small kegs of whiskey to the front lines to comfort the injured and those suffering from shock. As stretcher-bearers, they carried the wounded in wagons to the nursing camps. Moreover, they worked as scavengers, roaming the battlefields during the night, stripping the dead of their uniforms, caps and shoes. These uniforms were often dyed for *Cortinista* soldiers and civilians who needed them.[1]

Juan N. Cortina

Around the turn of the century, Canales had the opportunity to speak personally to two *Aguilas Damas*, both of whom were over the age of sixty at the time of the interview. They were now thin, hollow-checked women with pale and strained faces. Yet Canales found a mystery about them:

> *These women retained an Aguilas dignity; a timeless nobility still clung about them . . . They actually carried an undying bitterness, a bitterness too deep for words. Rarely would their soft-spoken words express the murder of their families and friends by the Gringo soldiers during the conflicts along the Rio Grande.*[2]

According to the interviews, one well known *Aguila* was "Lora La Leona" (Lora the Lion). Initially a spy, she became an advisor to Cortina and eventually an administrator. She assisted in keeping operations running efficiently and discreetly. Her office was furnished with plush upholstered furniture, heavy velvet draperies and gilded French mirrors with elaborate frames. Because of her prominence, she was often identified incorrectly as Cortina's mistress.[3] General William Steele recorded in 1875, "It is a well-known fact that not only Cortina himself, but even his mistress, gives orders to judges as to their decisions in cases, either civil or criminal and such orders are obeyed."[4] The people whom Canales interviewed in 1905 remembered Lora warmly. One said, "She was extremely well-read, a quick and witty conversationalist; Lora loved politics."[5]

Another *Aguila Dama*, Carmen Flores, helped secure funds for weapons and medicines at various locations throughout the region. She maintained a low profile, dressing like a witch in an aged, fading oversized black dress, beneath which she carried money or supplies sewn into her petticoats. According to accounts, "Like Lora, Carmen Flores had a sense for business, and both women had financial interests in several enterprises along the lower Rio Grande...[6] Their enterprises and talents served the *Cortinista* agenda.

An *Aguila Dama* remembered only as "Alma," discovered that a supposedly harmless and well-meaning local teacher named McMahan was actually supplying the Texas Rangers with information about the *Cortinistas*. "After gathering enough evidence revealing McMahan as a spy and saboteur, Alma turned him in to other Aguilas."[7] In June of 1875, McMahan "was found horribly mutilated, the head, arms, and legs being severed from the body and scattered over the prairie."[8] Frank Pierce wrote, "these men tortured McMahan by cutting off his fingers, toes, wrists and ears. They finally severed his legs from his body and left him lifeless."[9] This atrocity was done under the command of *aguja* [the needle]. According to Canales, this degree of violence was not unusual: "Most Aguilas were equally brutalized by McNally's troops and McMahan was one of those who had tortured some Mexicans."[10] It was later learned that McMahan "had been in fact a Brownsville policeman."[11] According to one of Canales interviews, "McNally's state troops,"[12] as W. Whipple referred to them, "had many clashes with the Cortinistas, in one of which Alma was killed."[13] The truth about her death, and that of most other *Cortinistas*, will never be fully known, as the only records are the testimony of McNelly's men.

One entrepreneur in the *Cortinista* cause was Gregoria Herrera. As a hotel keeper in Bagdad, she hid her political feelings so as to act as a spy for the *Cortinista* cause. She was always in close contact with two *Aguilas*, Antonio Villarreal and Manuel Luna, both of whom were stage drivers. Her hotel was a valuable spot from which to spy since the stage line stopped there. One account noted, "Saloons and hotels operated at full capacity. There were ten stagecoaches daily between Brownsville and Bagdad."[14] Cortina depended on her to keep records on the movement of Confederate, French and Union vessels and military officers. According to the research of Jose Canales, "Somehow she survived the sacking of Bagdad by numerous armies that almost destroyed the area."[15]

The *Aguila* officers were now more or less acquainted with the tactics of their enemies, and responded accordingly. As the violence persisted, each side kept improving its army and new maneuvers had to be created. Both sides saw the lower Rio Grande turmoil as a long, bitter war, in which neither side dared to make a fatal mistake. According to Canales, "It developed into a rigid, hard pounding conflict that was not fighting for peace, but to finally destroy the adversary once and for all. It brought bitter agony and endless sorrow to both sides."[16] Women were all but immune to the violence of the struggle. Most females who aided the *Cortinista* cause, suffered in deep silence. In winters, they lined their old dresses with rags or with bundles of newspapers to keep out the wind. They made shoes from carpets with soles of wood. These unknown, hard, bronze faced attendants molded bullets and provided military supplies. They carried on with a dignity that Cortina greatly admired. They toiled long hours as cooks, burning blisters on their fingers. They prepared hundreds of daily meals which left them with endless greasy, dirty dishes to scrub. Even though their hands were swollen and bruised they diligently washed and mended the men's torn and smudged clothes. Always walking with their heads held high, these women never complained regardless of their trials or tribulations. With reddish and puffy eyes, they worked with an earnest and simple face. These women who were called *burras*, a term that does little justice to their contribution, were indifferent to their own hunger and remained serene regardless of aching muscles and tension.[17]

"Angels of Mercy"

A majority of these *burras* were *Cortinista* wives or widows. They served as nurses. Some of them were *curanderas* (healers). They needed nerves of steel to handle foul, naked men who bore terrible war injuries, such as gangrene, a broken jaw, a leg or an arm gone, missing fingers or blindness. These soldiers groaned from pain in the intense summer heat that added to their ailments. They fell victim to flies, mosquitoes and gnats that further tormented them. Like most other soldiers throughout the South, these men also suffered from typhoid fever, pneumonia, diphtheria and malaria.[18] Most soldiers were also victims of polluted water.[19]

The *curanderas* mission was noble and humanitarian. One surgeon noted that the soldiers would be "burning with fever, tormented with insatiable thirst, racked with pains, or wild with delirium; their parched lips, and teeth blackened with sores, the hot breath and sunken eyes, the sallow skin and trembling pulse, all telling of the violent workings of these diseases."[20] With personal intensity, these women treated *Cortinista* troops and even wounded or ill French soldiers in Matamoros. With Juan Cortina's encouragement, these Mexican nurses and *curanderas* also attended to the Union or the Confederate soldiers in Brownsville. A large, red brick house with green shutters and two story veranda that belonged to Judge Israel Bigelow became a hospital during the Civil War. Crippled and weary soldiers carved their names or symbols on the wooden floors and on the woodwork. Several of these men waited to suffer the knives of surgeons. Others lingered in agony to face amputations. They depended on the *curanderas* to get drugs to ease pains.

Canales recalled that "these aching, sweat-drenched *burras* were actually angels of mercy, working in the wee hours of the soft, warm night. Long torches burned serenely like altar candles. These women were gentle, cheerful and sympathetic, masking their indignation and despair. They walked around with iron stomachs to witness the endless misery and to weather the rotten odors that assaulted their nostrils, primarily when they had to clean maggots from festering flesh. If nothing else they had to wash their patients to get rid of the lice, bandage wounds or stumps."[21] Canales recounted meeting one of these ladies: "Years later, I remembered talking to one of these *burras*. She had dark blazing, self-confident eyes set deep in a serene face. She triumphed over life with a dry humor even though she witnessed so much infirmity and grief. Like so many of these women, even in their youth, she appeared haggard and older than her years. Her eyes appeared deep. While looking into those eyes, my soul almost plunged into her spiritual self. I sensed an everlasting tranquility."[22] To these medical attendants, time stood still. These women had no past, no present, no future. Not even nerve-shattering sounds could disrupt their composure. They were immune to the daily agitations of life. They had seen everything and experienced just about everything; nothing appalled or unnerved them. Their large, dark eyes held the history of a people who for years witnessed all the tragedies that life had to offer.

A variety of pre-Columbian drugs were used by these women and men who were healers of pain. Apparently, several American doctors were impressed with their work, particularly when a Mexican healer saved the life of General James Shields during the Mexican War. As Samuel Schmucker noted, "His case had been given over as hopeless by the regular surgeons of the army, when a Mexican doctor offered to save his life if he would permit him to operate. The permission was readily granted."[23] The officer recovered when the doctor (healer) used a fine silk handkerchief to remove blood from his lungs. Canales believed that the mysterious doctor actually used medical herbs.

The *curanderas* treated soldiers suffering from burns or infections with *nopal* (cactus) juice and the juice of several other plants, together with honey and egg yolk. They also used jinson weed (datura) for burns and inflammations. Some of the seeds were used to induce visions and explore the inner mind for emotional problems. Although some thought they were witches, Cortina and his soldiers cherished these healers. No one trusted the local doctors. As the Austrian officer Ernst Pitner wrote in his diary, "Of all the four or five persons availing themselves of this title, not a single one is a real doctor. All in fact are nothing but quacks."[24]

Most physicians in the United States during the Civil War used the same treatments as the Mexican healers. Quinine, produced from the bark of the South American cinchona tree, was used with whiskey to treat headaches, toothaches, syphilis and fevers. Like the *burras*, these American physicians used opium and morphine to control diarrhea.[25] The *curanderas* knew about the concept of germs. They realized that scrubbing their hands and boiling instruments helped with their treatments, particularly when they had to remove bullets or perform operations. They saved soldiers' legs from amputation with their skillful treatment and herbs.

According to Jose Canales, "These nurses would all dress alike in black garments. They appeared like nuns, and lapsed into silence when someone approached them. One could sense their nerve and cunning skills in handling the unexpected. They had a quick, penetrating look and could read one's face like an open book. No detail escaped their scrutiny." People treated them with great respect since they were a critical part of the *Cortinista* survival.[26] The women who fought for, died for, and helped the *Cortinista* cause were an important reason for the survival of *Tejano* resistance along the Rio Grande. Their contributions were essential to the success of the rebellion. These courageous *Tejanas* were precursors of later *soldaderas* who would take part in the Mexican Revolution. While much remains to be written, some works already begin to shed light on the enormous contributions of Mexican American women in this period.

1. This practice was also common during the American Civil War. About 1863, a Virginia soldier wrote in his diary that "all the Yank dead had been stripped of every rag of their clothing and looked like hogs that had been cleaned. It was an awful sight." William K. Goolrick, The Civil War: Rebels Resurgent, Fredericksburg to Chancellorsville (Alexandria: Time-Life, 1985), 88.

2. Canales Interview, August 12, 1964.

3. Ibid.

4. W.M. Steele to the Adjutant General, July 1, 1875, "Texas Frontier Troubles," 122.

5. Canales Interview, November 16, 1964.

6. Ibid.

Juan N. Cortina

7. Ibid.

8. Report of the Brownsville Committee, April 17, 1875, "Texas Frontier Troubles," 58.

9. Pierce, A Brief History, 108.

10. Canales Interview, November 16, 1964.

11. Affidavit of Joseph O'Shaughnessy, June 16, 1875, "Texas Frontier Troubles," 82.

12. Whipple to the Adjutant General, November 20, 1875, in ibid., 89.

13. Canales Interview, November 16, 1964.

14. Stambaugh, Lower Rio Grande Valley, 112. For more data on Gregoria Herrera see Raybum, Centuries of Conflict, 72-77.

15. Canales Interview, November 16, 1964.

16. Ibid.

17. Ibid.

18. See George T. Stevens, Three Years in the Sixth Corps (Albany: S.R. Gray, Publishers, 1866), 10,114. He was a surgeon. Cholera also took its toll. See the San Antonio *Herald*, October 16,1866. In November 1, 1866, the *Herald* reported that the cholera epidemic "can be partially traced to the Mexican population who cannot protect itself from the rains..." In September, 1866, 116 Mexicans died from diseases. Also yellow fever swept the border several times, particularly in 1882. See Pierce, 137.

19. Stevens, 114. Foul water remained a problem. the San Antonio *Express*, October 25, 1878, stated that Mexicans depended on "contaminated water for cooking, drinking, and other purposes."

20. Stevens, 74.

21. Ibid.

The house of Judge Israel Bigelow, the first elected chief justice of Cameron County, remained standing in Brownsville for years until it was razed recently. For a photo of the house see: Ruby A. Wooldridge and Robert B. Vezzetti, Brownsville: A Pictorial History (Norfolk: Donning Company, 1982), 59.

Las Mujeres Cortinistas

22. Ibid.

23. Samuel Schmucker, A History of the Civil War in the United States with a Preliminary View of its Causes (Philadelphia: Bradley & Co., 1864), 316.

24. Pitner, 138.

25. David Nevin, The Civil War: Sherman's March: Atlanta to the Sea (Alexandria: Time-Life, 1986), 106-107.

26. Canales interview, November 16, 1964.

CHAPTER XI

The Final Years of Juan Cortina

Incredibly the *Cortinista* movement survived the turbulent years of the American Civil War and the French Occupation of Mexico. Cortina had wisely managed always to position himself where instead of been trampled by superior forces he became a key factor to their success. But now the wars were over and as the aging general was ready to address old grievances, he found new and formidable enemies among his former allies. Both the Mexican and American governments, in order to pursue economic and political self interests, would at all cost try to thwart the popular general.

In July 1875, under pressure from the United States, Mexican President Sebastian Lerdo arrested Cortina. He was accused of shipping stolen cattle and imprisoned near Mexico City. A report on Cortina's arrest by the Mexican Border Commissioners, later concluded "many in Brownsville were eager to involve General Cortina in cattle stealing whether he was guilty or not."[1] If there was to be no more unrest, the popular leader had to be contained one way or another. Almost a year later, on May 18, 1876, Cortina, who never went to trial nor ever received a hearing from President Lerdo, escaped from Mexico City. By 1877, the feared leader of the *Cortinistas* was again in the lower Rio Grande region. Servando Canales (no relation to J.T. Canales) an old enemy of Cortina and supporter of the Diaz government, was now the military governor of Tamaulipas.[2] Despite his own initial support of the Diaz Government, Cortina was apprehended by the military governor, quickly tried by martial court and ordered shot.[3]

Upon learning of Cortina's sentence, Sabas Cavazos, Cortina's half brother, went to Mexico and interceded with Diaz for Cortina's life. Diaz acceded and "immediately despatched Colonel *El Chato*

Juan N. Cortina

Garza and Lieutenant Colonel Felipe de Montenegro to Bagdad with
orders to General Servando Canales to deliver Cortina to the city of
Mexico."[4] Of Cortina's arrest John Ford commented, "I myself
commanded the escort which took Cortina who was then *encapillado*
(no one was allowed to speak to him) from the capella to Bagdad, and
delivered him to Colonel Garza on board the Libertad."[5] Cortina was
imprisoned in a gloomy old prison called Santiago Tlatelolco near
Mexico City.[6] There, isolated from his family and colleagues, Cortina
was held incommunicado and without legal representation.[7] The
dampness and meager scraps of spoiled food ruined his health, but not
his spirit. From prison he still ran many of his affairs. He was released
from prison in 1878, but was still confined to the Mexico City region.
Obviously the Mexican government intended to keep him far away
from the Rio Grande.

In the spring of 1890, an aging Cortina was allowed to visit
Matamoros in the company of his young wife. President Porfirio Diaz
paid for a lavish banquet in Cortina's honor. At the feast, Cortina
made amends and forgave his old enemies, such as Adolphus
Glavecke, eating with them at the same table. At the banquet, guests
saw a fatigued and aged man. His forehead showed delicate furrows
and his beard covered his cheekbones. Those who came to see him
knew that they would never again see their old leader, their last
opportunity to see a man who had literally made history. After a few
days Cortina went back to Mexico City. In 1891, he was officially
paroled to the limits of Mexico City. He was to be close, where Diaz
could keep close tabs on him.

The fate of the general was not only of interest to those of the
lower Rio Grande, but to many across the United States as well. In
1893, the New York *Times* reported that:

*A great sensation has been created by the telegraphic
announcement from the City of Mexico that General Juan
Cortina, one of the greatest revolutionary leaders of Mexico,
has been arrested and imprisoned in the San Juan Ulua (sic)*

*Prison by order of President Diaz for attempting to incite
another revolutionary uprising against the government. The
city of Matamoros (sic) is General Cortina's old home. He
was, twenty-five years ago, a desperate and greatly feared man
in Mexico. He ruled the Rio Grande border country from
Laredo to the mouth of the River . . . His influence was so great
that he could inaugurate a powerful revolutionary movement by
a single pronunciamento with his signature attached. His
exploits at the time of the Civil War caused the United States
Government to lose many thousands of dollars. When
President Diaz's revolution ended in success, General Cortina
was summoned to the City of Mexico . . . [Cortina] has been in
constant surveillance by President Diaz ever since to prevent
him from inciting further revolutions.*[8]

Now an old man, Cortina had again been imprisoned by Diaz
"because of his sympathies with the recent movement of Catarino
Garza," another militant *Tejano* who was thought to be instigating
revolution in south Texas.[9] He was released from San Juan de Ulloa
on February 17, 1894 and went back to Mexico City.[10] These series
of arrests attest to President Diaz's preoccupation with Cortina's
influence. When Cortina was released from his latest incarceration,
Jose Canales saw his uncle and interviewed him extensively. Canales
realized that Cortina was critically ill and it would probably be the last
time he would see the old warrior. Apparently Cortina enjoyed seeing
his nephew. He liked the small presents Canales brought, as well as
family gossip, local news, jokes and stories. At night Canales read the
newspaper for Cortina and they discussed politics. Canales humored
Cortina during his uncle's illness.

The media was in constant vigil of Cortina's health. On March
2, 1894, newspapers noted that Cortina's health was deteriorating
"General Juan Cortina is said to be at death's door."[11] Later the
newspaper commented, "Gen. Juan N. Cortina, of border notoriety,
who was given up by physicians, has rallied."[12] The newspaper

133

reported that Cortina was "out of danger" and that he would "continue to make life interesting for the guards of Mexico City which is his prison."[13] On October 30, 1894, at the age of 70, Cortina finally succumbed to pneumonia. Canales was surprised when he heard that Diaz had plans for an elaborate funeral for Cortina, whose body now rested in a white satin casket. Cortina received a military funeral with gallant soldiers and several trumpeters standing at attention and an officer delivering an emotional eulogy. Canales personally thought that his uncle was better off to die there than in Texas which still had contempt for him.[14] Juan N. Cortina was buried in the Panteon de Dolores near Mexico City

The Brownsville *Herald* noted about Cortina: "That his memory will long be cherished and cursed on the lower Rio Grande, there is no doubt, for if some people have cause to love him because of his former kindly acts, others have equal cause to hate him because of his evil deeds. Cortina was never a saint, but with his evil nature there was a certain amount of good, and the poor people loved him because of the charity he used to bestow."[15]

Juan Cortina's death brought to a close an incredible era. Times had changed leaving the *Cortinistas* with no allies on either side of the border. As Rodolfo Acuña observed, "The Anglo forces had no success against Cortina, but during the 1870s, as United States political influence with the Mexican government increased, pressure was brought to eliminate him."[16] Foreign capital wanted a strong, stable, and a peaceful Mexico under Diaz. Later in 1910, efforts were made by Jose Esparza, Jose Canales and other relatives to transport Cortina's body to Texas next to the grave of his mother on the family ranch near Brownsville. The turbulent Mexican Revolution and later the Great Depression ended that project. The blueprint of a marble monument depicting a sculptured angel comforting Cortina ended up in a drawer.[17]

Musical Tributes

With the passage of time, *corridos* (ballads) commemorated the *Cortinistas* and their leader. Folklorist and historian Americo Paredes concluded, "The lower border produced its first *corrido* hero, Juan Nepomuceno Cortina, in the late 1850s. . .That the Mexican *corrido* went through its first stages on the lower Rio Grande border-under the impulse of border conflict-is a thesis that could never be definitely proved."[18] Moreover, Professor Jose Limon noted: "From the 1860s until the turn of the century, heroic *corridos* about such encounters (the *Cortinistas*) began to appear in large numbers along the lower border."[19] Several of the *corridos* were shaped into *alabanzas* (hymns of praise) that contained joyful chants about overcoming suppression on earth or in the heavenly hereafter. Canales noted that some *alabanzas* failed to make sense to the uninformed ear. But they consisted of coded references to secret meetings, special events, or planned battles. Here is one fragment:

> *I bring my sorrow on heaven to bear*
> *To meet my Lord and have influence there*
> *I cry, I pray to dare.*
> *We seek love and victory there*
> *Let us unite to appreciate heaven well*
> *To remove ourselves from this earth hell.*[20]

Well into the 1920s some field hands still sang the *alabanzas* that had been common before battle. Here is a verse fragment:

> *We shall march with God*
> *Under Cheno's banner*
> *With the angels of love and faith*
> *To gain all hope*
> *To end suffering and despair*

135

Juan N. Cortina

> *Long live our cause*
> *In God we pray and strive*[21]

One of the most celebrated *corridos* was "The Night Ride of the *Fieles*." It included violins and trumpets accompanying a humorous account of the *Fieles*, fully dressed on horseback, falling into a canal. Canales remarked, "You could hear that one in every beer tavern in Brownsville during the warm summer nights. The music blasted down the streets . . . It was a long *corrido* that had several versions and was still renowned until World War I."[22] Later a condensed version was popularized by musicians Narcisco Martinez and Santiago Almeida in 1925. During the 1930s folklorists John and Alan Lomax recorded songs and stories of the Southwest, but almost nothing about Cortina. It was not until the 1950s that scholar Americo Paredes collected some fragments of *Cortinista corridos.* Paredes penned, "Cortina definitely is the earliest border *corrido* era that we know of, whether his exploits were put into *corridos* in 1860 or later."[23] Maria del Jesus Cisneros, a great aunt of Paredes, was born in 1850, and recalled *corridos* on the Cortina theme before she was ten, which indicates the songs were being sung in the late 1850s.[24] But it proved almost impossible for Paredes to find and record any complete versions; too many generations had passed and the songs had never been written down.

Some of the Chicano *corridos* on the *Cortinistas* were utilized as the background theme for plays. One play started as a personal narrative of a *Cortinista* trooper, telling about his battle while the *corrido* accompanied his story. The *corrido* was twisted to suit the time and the temperament of the audience. One actor played the part of the soldier's conscience. Two other troops came in with musical instruments to join him. The three warriors then prepare to fight the enemy with their lyrics of courage. After the ballad, women singers in white gowns joined the veterans and the play ended with an *alabanza.*[25]

Another theatrical performance was based on an old Spanish play, *"Los Moros y Cristianos."* The theme was changed to center on the *Cortinistas* and the Texas Rangers. A *Cortinista* leader, to the beat of drums, marched around a fort, singing for victory while his men listened. The *Cortinista* sends word to a Ranger captain that there will be no truce until one or the other is vanquished. After more singing, both forces engage in battle. When the *Cortinistas* triumphed over the Rangers, they recited an *alabanza* or a prayer of thanksgiving. The Ranger captain then humbled himself before a cross to pray for forgiveness and to be set free. The *Cortinistas* grant his request in the name of justice and the cross. Then music is heard and the play ends. On the stage, *cuentos* (folk stories) were presented by several actors telling different parts of the story. *Corridos* of the *Aguilas* were centered on religious topics like *"Camino del Calvario."* An *Aguila* hero would pray to Christ and Mary to forgive him in his world of brutality. There were also nursery rhymes on the *Aguilas*. One was based on *Don Gato*. The *Aguila* was the cat and the mice were the French soldiers.[26]

Interest in Cortina *corridos* surfaced in 1972, when the Chicano militant Brown Berets, dressed in uniforms and carrying flags, marched to Brownsville in search of the Cortina legacy. They erected a monument to him but found little awareness of Cortina among the populace.[27] Brown Beret leader David Sanchez stated:

I went around town asking about Juan Cortina who played an historical role in Brownsville about a hundred years ago. Some people knew of him, but the majority of people I talked to had never heard of him. Our research led us to an older lady by the name of Teresa Canales. She and her brother were relatives of Juan Cortina. J.T. Canales was an historian.[28]

If nothing concrete came of the Brown Beret inquiries, at least they revived curiosity in Juan Cortina, his time, and his movement, among the younger Chicano population. In the 1970s, the controversial Jose Angel Gutierrez became fascinated with Cortina. Pointing to the exploitation of *Tejanos* by the Anglo establishment, Gutierrez argued "that not since the turbulent years of *guerrillero* Juan 'Cheno' Cortina had Chicanos in Texas [had] been willing to challenge the Gringo power structure...." [29] Gutierrez had thus generated more interest in Cortinista *corridos*. A gifted *corrido* composer, Rumel Fuentes created "*Corrido de Juan Cortina*" in 1972.[30] Also the talented playwrite Luis Valdez promoted his own interpretation of Cortinista *corridos* with elements of Aztec culture and folklore. They were used in several of his short plays, divided into *actos* (short, improvised scenes).[31] Musicians like San Antonio's Emilio Navaira molded this border legacy that mushroomed beyond Texas borders.[32] In this way the legendary Juan Cortina was kept alive in the memory of the people.

1. Reports of the Mexican Border Commission, 62.

2. The San Antonio *Express*, February 11,1877, reported that Cortina was still active in military activities in Mexico. Then on February 28, 1877, it stated that dispatches from Brownsville revealed that Cortina fell from the good graces of Diaz.

3. Ibid. During this era, another Chicano, Tiburcio Vasquez also was facing trial in San Benito County, California. As he said, "I know that the people of said county en mass are so prejudiced a conviction that I am guilty of the crimes charged in said indictment and of a multitude of others not charged... .1 am so assured of this state of feeling and of this determination to hang me for my bad name... .This statement is not the confession of cowardice but of a conviction that unrestrained public rage has no heart as it has no ears." Quoted from California Courts District, Court 20th Judicial District: The people . . .versus Tiburcio Vasquez, August 2?, 1874, Hollister, Calif. (translated] H M 26615.
    Like Carlos Esparra, Vasquez loved to read Spanish classics. He wrote in a letter, "Yesterday, Thursday, I received the book titled <u>Don Quixote de Ia Mancha</u> from the hands of a gentleman to whom I returned the other two books.[4] Tiburcio Vasquez to C.B. Darwin, November 7, 1874. [translated] H M 26624. Both documents are in the Huntington Library, San Marino, Calif.

4. John Ford, "Some Historical Facts," Brownsville *Herald*, March 4, 1893. "One must read this account with skepticism," Canales asserted. In fact, as the editors noted: "The final paragraph of this letter being entirely of a personal nature, and not having bearing on the historical facts," had to be omitted.

The Final Years of Juan Cortina

Canales explained that a few years later he became friendly with the editor of the newspaper and said that the newspaper needed to censor Ford's glorification of himself and his loathing of Cortina.

5.   Ford, "Some Historical Facts," Brownsville *Herald*, March 4,1893.

6.   San Antonio *Express*, April 24,1877, stated that Cortina was arrested by Mexican authorities and transferred to Mexico City.

7.   One argument for Cortina's arrest was that his political ideas would not conform to the Diaz government's internal and foreign policy. It is ironic how history repeats itself. One can see this in the 1992 case of Agapito Gonzalez Cavazos, leader of the Union of Journeymen and Industrial Workers in Matamoros. Cavazos, unlike most of the union leadership, has been aggressive with American-owned companies. "In negotiations early in 1992, he sought an increase of wages for his union membership to bring them up to $1.74 an hour. The companies, unhappy with his aggressive negotiating style, sent their Mexican lawyer to complain to President Carlos Salinas de Gotari that Cavazos was mining the investment climate in Matamoros," said Jerome I. Levinson, an attorney and special adviser to the president of the Inter-American Development Bank. Within days of the meeting with Salinas, Cavazos was arrested and taken to Mexico City, where he was held incommunicado and grilled by two magistrates about alleged tax evasion in 1988. Without a lawyer present and isolated from his family and union colleagues, this 76-year-old man began to hyperventilate. He was transferred to a hotel, then removed to a hospital, remaining under arrest the entire time. "The message was clear: Conform to the governments low-wage policy or pay the price. The Cavazos case is not an aberration; it is symptomatic of the state of labor relations in Mexico." See J. Levinson, "Give Mexican Workers Their Due," Los Angeles *Times*, September 29, 1992.

8.   New York *Times*, November 18, 1893.

9.   Brownsville *Herald*, March 10, 1894.

10.   Brownsville *Herald*, February 17, 1894.

11.   Brownsville *Herald*, March 2, 1894.

12.   Brownsville *Herald*, March 9, 1894.

13.   Brownsville *Herald*, March 12, 1894.

14.   Canales Interview, November 16, 1964.

15.   Brownsville *Herald*, March 10, 1894.

139

Juan N. Cortina

14. Canales Interview, November 16, 1964.

15. Brownsville *Herald*, March 10, 1894.

16. Acuña, Occupied America, 47. The Brownsville *Herald*, March 10,1894, stated that Cortina "possessed a large amount of common sense, and he was also a good judge of men." The article went on to say that he is now a "very old man, bowed and bent by the weight of years... and had been placed in a Mexican prison by Diaz because of his sympathies with the recent movement of Catarino Garia." Goldfinch, Cortina, 62-63, related how Ford saved Cortina from being shot by General Servando Canales. "This is another Ford myth that is hard to erase," said J.T. Canales. See also, Miguel Angel Peral, Diccionario Biografico Mexicano (Mexico, D.F.: Editorial P.A.C., 1944), 191.
Cortina's exile took place due to major political changes in Mexico. "With the growth of technology and the reform of the army, the centrifugal forces of *caudillismo* gave way before the strength of the central government. All the powerful local chiefs... either had to accommodate growing national power or face the military might of the state." By 1876, all but one of these powerful local chiefs--Porfirio Diaz--would "either be completely subordinate to the national government or dead." See Richard N. Sinkin, The Mexican Reform, 1855-1876: A Study in Liberal Nation-Building (Austin: University of Texas Press, 1979), 105, 112-13.

17. The author has a copy of the drawing. Jose Esparza, the father of the author's grandmother, Francisca Esparza Montalvo, had given $5,000 for the project. Other people raised money for the lavish, marble monument. Due to the Great Depression during the 1930s, the money was given instead for public relief.

18. Americo Paredes, Folklore and Culture on the Texas-Mexican Border (Austin: University of Texas Press, 1993), 140-141.

19. Jose E. Limon, Mexican Ballads, Chicano Poems: History and Influence in Mexican-American Social Poetry (Berkeley: University of California Press, 1992), 24.

20. Canales Interview, November 16, 1964. These *corrido* fragments were translated into English by Canales. He did not focus much on *corridos*. His interest was law and history. As a religious man, the *alabanzas* intrigued him.

21. Ibid.

22. Ibid.

23. Americo Paredes, "With his Pistol in his hand:" A Border Ballad and its Hero (Austin: University of Texas Press, 1958), 140. What the Texas border needs is a cultural survey of integrating folklife and historic preservation. For example the

model of Thomas Carter and Carl Fleischhauer, The Grouse Creek Cultural Survey (Washington: Library of Congress, 1988), in Utah could be used. Recently some folk music from Texas has been preserved in the Library of Congress. For example the music of Leonardo "Flaco" Jimenez is now collected for its folklore center. The Jimenez family has been active on the border for generations. Still most of this border music remains unknown since it seldom appears in record shops and catalogs. For more on this topic see: American Folk Music and Folklore Recordings: A Selected List (Washington: Library of Congress, 1987). As for the Lomax recordings, see Lamar, Readers Encyclopedia, 674-675.

24.   Ibid., 139.

25.   Canales Interview, August 24, 1964. This data was gathered from about 1898 to 1910. Canales met several singers who were involved with these *corridos* who shared their reflections with him. Yet Canales was limited since he had no understanding of performance practices, stylistic features, vocal or instrumental combinations or even melodic structures.

26.   Canales compared his *corrido* material with one of his favorite books: Aurora Lucero-White Lea, Literary Folklore of the Hispanic Southwest (San Antonio: The Naylor Company, 1953). Since Lea's work was religious by nature, Canales enjoyed her topic. He invited her to do a study on the folklore of the Lower Rio Grande and was to provide the funds. Apparently she did not accept his invitation. Canales knew her through her father, Antonio Lucero, first secretary of state for New Mexico. At one time or another, they worked together on civil rights for Hispanics.

27.   David Sanchez, Expedition Through Aztlán (La Puente, California: Perspectiva Press, 1978), 171.

28.   Ibid., 156.

29.   Armando Navarro, Mexican American Youth Organization: Avant-Garde of the Chicano Movement in Texas (Austin: University of Texas Press, 1995), 173-174. See also 182.

30.   The prolific Fuentes also composed "El Corrido de la Familia de Juan Corona," "El Corrido de George Sanchez," "Corrido de Aztlan," and numerous others. He composed about thirty *corridos*. Some of them were published in El Grito del Sol:A Journal of Contemporary Mexican-American Thought, Spring, 1973. See also "Corridos" in Austin *Echo*, November 9, 1973.

31.   For more on his work see Luis Valdez, Early Works: Actos Pensamiento Sementino and Bernabe (Houston: Arte Publico Press, 1990). Also for details on the meaning of *actos* see Jorge A. Huerta, "Chicano Teatro: A Background," Aztlán: Chicano Journal of the Social Sciences and the Arts, Fall, 1971, 67.

32.   See "Emilio Navaira Takes A Spin Down A Country Road," *Hispanic*, September, 1995, 35-36. See also 8.

CHAPTER XII

Conclusions: Reflections on Cortina

Following the conquest of what is present-day south Texas, Americans moved in and pursued their social and economic objectives with little or no consideration for the rights or welfare of the indigenous population. Mexicans were harassed, humiliated, robbed, raped, and murdered. Whatever protections was promised to them by American law or policy proved a mockery.[1] The *Cortinista* crusade evolved as a result of this treatment, giving expression to the indignation of a people. Cortina's fiery proclamations exposed the base motives of the invaders and attracted a large following among those who had lost their land, their families, their dignity, and their hope.[2]

The *Cortinista* campaign, for all of its notoriety and legendary discipline and organization, faced overwhelming odds in its struggle with the determination and military might of the state of Texas and the United States government. Cortina might have been more successful in achieving his goals and military objectives had he had the full support of the Mexican community in other parts of Texas. However, some *Tejano* leaders, such as Santos Benavides, failed to commit themselves to a united struggle, choosing instead to throw in with the Anglos in exchange for security and guarantees of respect for business and property.[3] Thus, in the process, some established Mexican businessmen assisted the American government in attempting to crush the *Cortinistas.*

Hostilities lingered over nearly three decades. A significant number of people, men and women, were willing to fight and die for what they believed in. Being a guerrilla warrior had its exhilarating moments, but most of the time was passed in corrosive anxiety and

143

dismal drudgery.[4] Some became victims of alcoholism, exhaustion, and shock, due to a constant state of warfare with little chance of a clear victory. Others were driven into reckless, brutal behavior which in the end would destroy them. What began as action, in pursuit of a noble cause, later became too violent for its own sake. Still, a majority retained a persistent dignity, an uncompromising gallantry to the cause. In the end, the American government inflicted cruel reprisals, and Cortina himself was captured by Mexican troops and exiled to central Mexico in 1877.[5]

Tejanos ultimately prevailed in this unhappy land of conflict and confusion. Yet, the lower Rio Grande remained haunted by instability and chronic social ills, mired deep in poverty with a lingering hatred for their reckless oppressors. Again they waited to topple their enemies, ready to engulf the region in chaos, if necessary. These *Tejanos* gathered valuable experience through the *Cortinista* struggle of 1848-1876. The *Cortinista* movement demonstrated the possibilities of mass resistance and provided a vehicle of expression and a source of inspiration. It laid the groundwork for subsequent resistance movements under Catarino Garza, Aniceto Pizaña, Luis de la Rosa, and, later, Jose Canales himself, all of which contributed to shaping present day relations not only in Texas but between the United States and Mexico.[6]

Cortina represented only a first effort to right wrongs against a *Tejano* community. T. R. Fehrenbach remarked, "But the evil that was spawned lived on; there was to be even more bloodshed on the Rio Grande."[7] Historian David Montejano also wrote, "Indeed, the Nueces strip of South Texas....remained 'untamed' for nearly fifty years after annexation. A frontier battalion of Texas Rangers, stationed in the border zone until 1920, represented the armed force of the Anglo-Texas order."[8] "Ugly tensions between the races remained as a legacy of the 'Cortina War.'" [9]

The fact that some scholars see Cortina only as a symbol of Hispanic culture fighting for survival in a superimposed and unsympathetic Anglo society does not make Cortina or his movement any less important or worthy of our attention. The political and sociological complexities of the period, and Cortina's numerous layered interests and involvements in three overlapping wars, constitute a challenging study of Mexican American history on different levels. Other historians persist in belittling the value of the Cortina legacy, such as, Manuel Machado's statement that "hotheads like Cortina, however, retarded attempts by both Anglos and Mexicans to achieve some sort of working relationship in Texas."[10] Matt S. Meier wrote, "Cortina's actions led to greater hatred of Mexicans and more persecution."[11]

But why do Machado, Meier and other Hispanic professors continue to deprecate the *Cortinistas*? One reason may rest in the Latin readiness "to praise the foreign and belittle their own, marked a kind of inferiority complex of the type that sometimes moves with popular currents. It could be likened, perhaps to the general American....cultural inferiority complex which so handicapped appreciation of the American scene in the nineteenth and early twentieth centuries, because it was always under the shadow of Europe."[12] This kind of mentality prevents exploring new concepts, and hinders original research and creates arrogance, inertia and an unwillingness to make progress. It encourages a denial of the importance of the *Cortinista* movement, thereby devaluing the struggle for civil rights itself, then and now. We also take away something from Latin American History, for as Octavio Paz observed, "Latin American history is simply the sum total of answers, each of them different, that we have given to this question put to us by our original condition."[13]

The Cortina quest awaits a fresh perspective from a new generation of writers, poets, and artists, historians and scholars. It is part of the Latino legacy, a history that belongs to a people who will comprise the largest minority in the United States in the 21st century. Historian Mario T. Garcia noted, "We must understand these profound ethnic and demographic changes and seek to learn from history what they will mean in a new ethnic era of the country."

145

Juan N. Cortina

Finally, the heritage of the Mexican American is not a foreign and alien episode, but a profoundly American experience.[14]

1. Reports of Mexican Border Commission, 130-148.

2. "Difficulties on Southwestern Frontier,"[4] 69-82. Newspapers stated bluntly that Cortinistas and other Chicanos were "natural thieves" that "live[d] in sinks, sewers and shanties." For references see the Brownsville *Ranchero*, May 25, 1868, May 29, 1869; San Antonio *Daily Express,* January 8, 1874; Galveston *Daily News*, February 8, December 17, 1868.

3. Dudley G. Wooten, A Comprehensive History of Texas 1665-1897 (Dallas; William G. Scarf (1898), Vol 11. Benavides did well. He was a member of the 16th, 17th and 18th legislatures. He went on to become a Texas Commissioner to the World's Cotton Exposition in 1884.

4. Canales Interview, November 16, 1964.

5. Ibid.

6. Montejano, Anglos and Mexicans in the Making of Texas, 89,126, 305.

7 Fehrenbach, Lone Star, 501. Also Gen E.O.C. Ord's report, October 1,1879, U.S. Congress House of Representatives, Annual Report of the Secretary of War for 1879, 46th Cong., 2nd Sess., House Exec. Doc., No 1, Pt 2, Vol.1, Serial 1903 (Washington, D.C., 1879), 90-93. Also see: San Antonio *Express*, November 18, 20, December 7, 1879.

8. Montejano, Anglos and Mexicans in the Making of Texas, 33.

9. Arnoldo De Leon, "Los Tejanos: An Overview of Their History," in Ben Procter and Archie P. McDonald, The Texas Heritage (St. Louis: Forum Press, 1980), 136.

10. Manuel A. Machado, Listen Chicano: An Informal History of the Mexican-American (Chicago: Nelson Hall, 1978), 36.

11. Matt S. Meier, Mexican American Biographies: A Historical Dictionary, 1836-1987 (New York: Greenwood Press, 1988), 68.

12. Powell, 111.

13. Octavio Paz, Convergences: Essays on Art and Literature (1987), 222.

Conclusions: Reflections on Cortina

14. Mario Garcia, Mexican American: Leadership. Ideology & Identity, 1930-1960 (New Haven: Yale University, 1989), 302.

Hispanics still need to know more about their rich legacy in order to have a positive image about themselves. There are numerous Chicanos who suffered from a lack of understanding of their history. For example, the gifted writer Richard Rodriguez is still trying to learn about his heritage and has questions about it. His writings are marred with this complex issue. Still his prose is to be admired. As one critic noted, Rodriguez is "a lyrical essayist who can match... Albert Camus for sheer talent." See Bettijane Levine, "A Work in Progress: At 48, Richard Rodriguez is Still Struggling with Questions About His Heritage," Los Angeles *Times*, November 9, 1992.

Appendix A

An Essay on Sources:
Cortina and the Historians

Doing research on Juan Cortina, and the Mexican community in general during the period 1850-1910, presents a number of challenges. One obstacle is that scholars who research this period are likely to find a very limited amount of data, and documentation particularly on such important topics as the *Aguilas Negras, Los Fieles de Cortina*, and the *Exploradores*.[1] Another problem is that those documents which are found often only recount the testimonies of people who are anti-Mexican and anti-*Cortinistas*. Both the Mexican community and the *Cortinistas* are consistently portrayed as cattle thieves and murderers.[2]

These stereotypes clearly represent popular sentiment of the time making it risky to rely on contemporary sources of that era. For example, regional newspapers such as The *Ranchero* (Corpus Christi, Matamoros and Brownsville), the San Antonio *Express*, and the San Antonio *Herald* perpetuated negative stereotypes. In numerous references to the *Cortinistas*, these newspapers expressed Hispanophobic views to an uncritical constituency already steeped in similar prejudice.[3] Other publications were no less biased. In 1870 Thomas North wrote this of the *Cortinistas* in his narratives: "We will here record a tragic incident to illustrate the savage character of this half-breed, semi-barbarian Cortinas."[4] Later, in 1894, Mary M.

149

Brown penned a popular textbook on the history of Texas. In her work she wrote of how the Rio Grande frontier was "harassed by a band of armed Mexicans and Indians under the Mexican Chief Cortina." Somehow, readers were left with the impression that Cortina was a Comanche.[5]

Renowned historian J. Fred Rippy was one of the first to attempt a more serious study on the Cortina Wars. His account was "based almost entirely upon primary material . . . newspapers . . . periodicals . . . documents published by two governments or drawn from their archives."[6] While Rippy might have taken a more academic approach, Cortina was once again labeled as a "chieftain" who did little more than commit depredations in Texas.

Still, a wealth of *Cortinista* material exists and if gathered and screened properly, it paints a more balanced picture of the *Cortinista* movement. The material however, is scattered from the National Archives in Mexico, to Yale University, to the Library of Congress in Washington, D.C.. In addition, much of this material is neither catalogued, labeled, nor cross-referenced.[7] *Cortinista* materials can also be found in the special collections of American Universities. The Archille-Francois Bazaine Archives, at the Benson Latin American Library, University of Texas, Austin, has a wealth of documents relating to Cortina. About 1890, a writer, Ernest Louet, formerly a finance officer with the French Army in Mexico, began a history of this period. He used what became known as the Bazaine papers and other important letters. According to resources, "He failed to complete his history; death overtook him shortly after he began."[8] Afterwards, the Bazaine papers were almost destroyed. Fortunately, they were rescued by the Mexican minister to Spain, Jesus Zenil, and, in 1906, the Mexican Minister of Foreign Affairs, Ignacio Mariscal, brought them to Mexico. Later, scholar Genaro Garcia acquired them and used them for his research. The documents were eventually purchased by the University of Texas as part of what became the Garcia Collection.

There are other sources, such as the Jose San Roman papers (1823-1934), at the Barker Texas History Center at the University of Texas, which shed some light on the *Cortinista* movement; but the papers have badly deteriorated with age.[9] For some unfathomable reason, the university refused to microfilm them.

Not to be forgotten is the material collected by Hubert Howe Bancroft. Bancroft's history factory, while much criticized, contains an abundance of material from that period, including documentation on Juan Cortina. For example, a letter written by Juan Cortina, dated 1862, surfaced in the Bancroft Library, University of California, Berkeley, in 1981, and there are undoubtedly more Cortina letters or documents still uncatalogued in this library.[10]

Unfortunately, many other important documents were destroyed or lost. For instance, Colonel Charles Dupin, French Provisional Governor of Tamaulipas (1864-1866), "caused all state archives to be destroyed."[11] In 1985, in an attempt to compensate for this historical disaster, Professor Mirabel Miro Flauquer of the Universidad Autónoma de Tamaulipas in Ciudad Victoria assembled those papers of Porfirio Diaz relating to Tamaulipas, which provide information on the last decade of Cortina's life. As is the case with other sources, the cautious scholar must view them with caution since Diaz was no friend of Cortina and like Ford, made every effort to discredit him for political reasons.[12]

Moreover, documents that were not destroyed were often altered for a number of reasons. For example, while the United States War Department's Official Records contain material on Cortina, the chief editor, Lieutenant Colonel Robert N. Scott, edited it according to his limited view and personal bias.[13] Historian Harold E. Mahan held that the chief editor distorted the truth: "He obscured much of the war's social reality . . . it de-emphasized the role of Blacks [and of Chicanos]."[14] Jose Canales believed that these editors mutilated some of the original Cortina documents by cutting out portions of them for ease of reference and organized by subject. [15] Canales had in his possession two original documents that he found altered in United States government publications. It is for these reasons that most primary documents are not available to the scholar today.

A tremendous quantity of primary documents on Juan Cortina has been lost. The original indictments against him are missing from the Cameron County Courthouse at Brownsville. According to other sources, "The number of the indictments seems to indicate that they were placed on the record book in 1848 at the time of the first meeting of the district court. The record book for the first meeting of the court has been damaged and some pages are probably missing."[16] The James Ross Browne reports (1854) on the *Aguilas Negras* were lost later in the century. Historian David M. Goodman wrote, "Only a fragment of one letter has survived from the additional reports Brown sent to Washington . . . for some reason these reports have been lost, misplaced, or removed from the National Archives."[17] The difficulty of obtaining data on the *Aguilas* could be attributed partially to that organization's own secrecy and to the reluctance of the United States government to document fully the trouble and embarrassment this group caused the government and the Texas Rangers.[18]

What records the *Aguilas* kept were also almost certainly destroyed in order to prevent opening wounds or shattering friendships. References to *Aguila* collaboration could have destroyed careers and reputations or could even have resulted in death. Embarrassing information was collected from homes, businesses and even the church confessionals.[19] Thus, the likelihood of finding such documents is remote indeed. Regarding the *Fieles de Cortina* and the *Exploradores*, Canales stated, "One must have the patience of a saint to study these mysterious organizations."[20] Canales was able to elicit reminiscences from a few *Aguilas*, but otherwise, people who might have had recollections to share have largely kept their silence.[21]

In short, while there is a considerable amount of literature on the *Cortinista* movement, most of the sources are limited to certain parts of the social conflict. In addition, the material tends to be highly insensitive to the Mexican community, if not completely biased. The writings of John Ford might best illustrate what the scholar will encounter in his or her quest to find out more about the *Cortinistas*. Ford is without a doubt a key primary source on the *Cortinistas*. He is also however, an individual who spent his life popularizing Hispanophobic biases. He viewed confrontations between Mexicans and Anglos in Texas as a contest between good and evil. As a general rule, he found excuses for the reckless behavior of Texas Rangers and other men, but condemned any *Cortinista* action. In this, Ford mirrors most writers of the time who failed to see in the *Cortinista* movement a struggle for social justice. Instead he and others tragically saw and documented the *Cortinista* political movement only as acts of "horse thieves and bandidos." Thus we are even more grateful to Canales for his foresight to interview and record the words of Cortina and those who took part in the struggle for justice in Texas.

Cortina's history is ever changing due to the discovery of new sources and to the reinterpretation of history by a new generation of historians. We hope that this work becomes one of many which brings new clarity to the life and times of Juan Cortina. It has been our objective to present Cortina and the *Cortinista* movement as part of a struggle for social justice and not simply as rebels without a cause as so many previous works have done. We sincerely hope that justice has and will be done.

1. Reports of Mexican Border Commission, 154-55, 158-159, contains the only extensive information known on the subject.

2. W.M. Steele to the Adjutant General, July 1, 1875, "Texas Frontier Troubles," 122; Douglas, "El Caudillo de La Frontera," 115.

3. These stereotypes were common in major newspapers. For example, Mexicans and Blacks were seen as "Living Curiosities at Barnum's Museum." As Frank Leslie's Illustrated Newspaper. December 15,1860, said, "They are freaks of nature... have excited equally the wonder of the learned and the unlearned... In the foreground are the Aztec children. . . It is likely they have been serving idols, for they are dumb as idols."

the Aztec children. . . It is likely they have been serving idols, for they are dumb as idols."

Another example is the sketch: "Dark Artillery; Or, How to Make the Contrabands Useful," October 26, 1861. Some "Dumb Niggers", with huge, wide lips, are bending over while holding cannons on their backs, firing at the rebels.

4.   North, 179.

5.   Mary M. Brown, A School History of Texas from its Discovery in 1685 to 1893 (Dallas; By the author, 1894), 37.

6.   Rippy, "Border Troubles Along the Rio Grande," viii.

7.   For example, a letter of Juan Cortina to Enrique Antonio Mexia (1829-1896), Matamoros, Tamaulipas, May 5, 1862, surfaced in the Bancroft Library, University of California, Berkeley in 1981. See Mexia Family Papers, 1894-1951, Portfolio, C-Miscellany, Box 2.

It illustrates Cortina's problems with grammar. There may be more Cortina's letters or documents uncatalogued in this library. The Manuscript Division of the Library of Congress, may contain documents relative to Cortina. See George H. Giddings Papers, Edward Lee Plumb Papers, and the Matthew Fontaine Maury Papers. For a guide to these archives see John R. Sellers, Civil War Manuscripts: A Guide to Collection in the Library of Congress (Washington: Library of Congress, 1986). To start with, see the index on "Mexico; Confederate agents in," 350.

Another indispensable guide for possible Cortina material is George S. Ulibarri and John P. Harrison, Guide to Materials on Latin America in the National Archives of the United States (Washington D.C.: National Archives and Records Administration, 1987), 44, 125, 161, 172. These materials have been overlooked by most historians.

8.   Dabbs, French Army in Mexico, 8.

9.   Archivist Chester V. Kielman wrote about the Jose San Roman archives: "Papers also relate to. . . threat of French occupation of Matamoros; military occupation of Matamoros by J. Cortina; blockade running of cotton, arms, drugs, and medicine for the Confederate States of America." Kielman, The University of Texas Archives (Austin: University of Texas Press, 1967), 315. Especially relevant are the José San Román Papers. When the author picked up some of these documents, they crumbled into fragments. However, most of the business correspondence of San Roman is in good condition. In Box 2G76, see: A. Vance to San Roman, February 23, 1865; In Box 2G77, see: W.S. Hanis to San Roman, November 28, 1865; Thomas C. Reynolds to San Roman, March 13, 1865; Manuel Peez to San Roman, April 19, 1866; S. Saldana to San Roman; S. Cavazos to San Roman, June 26, 1867. There were three

other letters of Sabas Cavazos that were fragments. In these boxes, the author saw about three or four letters written in "a mysterious code that was used by some of the Cortinistas." The author has a copy of one that is "a true and correct photocopy of 'secret coded document' in letters 1876 from San Roman Collection." Affidavit of Chester Kielman, April 21, 1977, Austin, Texas.

Thomas D. Schoonover studied "the vast body of manuscripts and printed source material" on the Mexican statesman Matias Romero. In some of these items there are references to Juan Cortina. See Schoonover's Mexican Lobby: Matias Romero in Washington. 1861-1867 (Lexington: University Press of Kentucky, 1986), 78, 162.

10. Priceless historical documents, even in the Bancroft Library, have never been catalogued. In 1952, for example, the library published a manuscript of California governor Leland Stanford, written by Hubert Bancroft. As Joseph A. Sullivan said: "We found the original manuscript, and as was customary the original contributions of the assigned writers of the History Company." Hubert Howe Bancroft, History of the Life of Leland Stanford: A Character Study (Oakland, California: BioBooks, 1952), iv.

Also, the original documents and the memoirs of Catarino E. Garza were never catalogued at the University of Texas. As of 1978, they were still not catalogued and some has been lost. Fortunately the library had a microfilm copy of Garza's work.

Another example of how materials are not catalogued, labeled or cross-referenced, can be seen in the Huntington Library, San Marino, California. World famous for some material on British and American culture, most of the items still have a gold or salmon color slip which means uncatalogued items.

In June 1991, when the author was admiring some rare 16th Century Mexican books in the Huntington, someone discovered a rare handwritten copy of a Christopher Columbus letter. "I don't think anybody realized at first how important it was," William Frank, the Huntington's associate manuscript curator said. "The letter was ignored in the library for more than 60 years." It was buried in a genealogical work about Portuguese royalty. For more details, see Larry Gordon, "Copy of Columbus is a Windfall," Los Angeles *Times*, July 10, 1991. As to cataloguing problems, see: A Guide for Readers: The Huntington Library (San Marino: Huntington Library, 1987), 6-8.

Also, Amy Wallace, "Huntington Library: Orderly Chaos but a Researcher's Delight," Los Angeles *Times*, May 11, 1992 "Half a million rare and reference books are shelved under 500 categories, some of them downright quirky." Lida Bushloper, the stacks supervisor, said. "Basically, you have to be a little old man who's worked here for 80 years to find anything." Most of their historical items are still stored in boxes. "Of all the stuff, only about one-tenth has yet been catalogued."

Major collections in most archives in Mexico are not catalogued, making it difficult to seek Cortinista data University of San Diego law professor Jorge Vargas is doing a study on California history through the National Archives of Mexico. He "estimates that less than 40% of Mexico's archives have been catalogued in large part because, until recently, they were scattered throughout the country and in various government ministries."

Vargas declared that the archives were consolidated after the nation's most notorious prison, Lecumberri Palace," "was dosed and its cellblocks remodeled with glass-covered ceilings and marble floors to hold the historical material." See David Smoller, "Law Professor Hunts Down State's History," Los Angeles *Times*, March 2, 1992.

Prior to 1934, the National Archives in Washington faced the same problem. The Director of Legislative Archives, Mike Gillette, said that no one is certain how many archives have been lost before the archives building was completed. "Before that, every federal agency in Washington kept its own attic, so to speak, and much was lost to fire, rain and thievery." See Geraldine Baum, "The Stuff America Is Made of, Boxes and Boxes of It," Los Angeles *Times*, March 3, 1992.

11. Stambaugh, Lower Rio Grande Valley, 126; Pierce, A Brief History, 56. See also Saldivar, Historia Tamaulipas, 8.

12. Mirabel Miro Flaquer, ed., Catálogo de Documentos-Carta de la Collección Porfirio Diaz-Tamaulipas. Marzo 1876-Noviembre 1885 (Ciudad Victoria: Universidad Autbnoma de Tamaulipas, 1985), Vols. I and 2.

13. Harold F. Mahan, "The Arsenal of History: The Official Records of the War of the Rebellion," Civil War History: A Journal of the Middle Period (March, 1983), 26.

14. Ibid.

15. Canales Interview, August 30, 1964.

16. Goldfinch, Cortina, 22-23.

17. David Michael Goodman, A Western Panorama 1849-1875: J. Ross Browne (Glendale: Arthur H. Clark Co., 1966), 47; Richard H. Dillon, J. Ross Browne, Confidential Agent in Old California (Norman: University of Oklahoma Press, 1965), xvi, 49.

18. Canales Interview, November 16, 1964.

19. The pursuit of the *Aguila Negra* records to prevent wrecking careers and saving reputations has a similar correlation with modem Germany. One can see the similarity with the former East German Ministry for State Security, the Stasi. This organization kept intimate, inane, details on at least one million people. The files are about 108 miles long. The data has "cut a swath through the eastern German psyche, destroying reputations, wrecking marriages, breaking friendships, ruining careers, and tarnishing idols."

German chancellor, Helmut Kohl, declared, "The Stasi files are an irritant. . . because they poison the entire atmosphere and because nobody knows exactly what material in them is fact and what's fiction. If I were fully free to decide, then I know exactly what should happen to those files." Friedrich Schorlemmer, and East German Protestant pastor and political activist, demanded that the files be closed in 1996 and "destroyed in a giant bonfire." What is ironic is that there was a familiar fate over a hundred years ago along the lower Rio Grande region with the *Aguila Negra* files. See Tyler Marshall, "Actor's Role As Informer Is Bit Part in German Tragedy," Los Angeles *Times*, December 28, 1993.

20. Ibid.

21. Canales Interview, November 16, 1964

157

Proclamation

Juan Nepomuceno Cortinas to the Inhabitants of the State of Texas and especially to those of the city of Brownsville.

These have connived with each other, and form, so to speak, a perfidious inquisitorial lodge to persecute and rob us without any cause, and for no other crime on our part than that of being of Mexican origin, considering us, doubtless, destitute of those gifts which they themselves do not possess.

To defend ourselves, and making use of the sacred right of self-preservation, we have assembled in a popular meeting with a view of discussing a means by which to put an end to our misfortunes.

The assembly organized, and headed by your humble servant, (thanks to the confidence which he inspired as one of the most aggrieved,) we have careered over the streets of the city in search of our adversaries, inasmuch as justice being administered by their own hands, the supremacy of the law has failed to accomplish its object. Some of them, rashly remiss in complying with our demand, have perished for having sought to carry their animosity beyond the limits allowed by their precarious position. Three of them have died-all criminal, wicked men, notorious among the people for their misdeeds. The others, still more unworthy and wretched, dragged themselves through the mire to escape our anger,

These, as we have said, form, with a multiple of lawyers, a secret conclave, with all its ramifications, for the sole purpose of despoiling the Mexicans of their lands and usurp(ing) them afterwards. This is clearly proven by the conduct of one Adolph Glavecke, who, invested with the character of deputy sheriff, and in collusion with the said lawyers, has spread terror among the unwary, making them believe that he will hang the Mexicans and burn their ranches, &c., that by this means he might compel them to abandon the country, and thus

159

accomplish their objcct. This is not a supposition-it is a reality, and notwithstanding the want of better proof, if this threat were not publicly known, all would feel persuaded that of this, and even more, are capable such criminal men as the one last mentioned, the marshal, the jailer, Morris, Neal, &c.

All truce between them and us is at an end, from the fact alone of our holding upon this soil our interests and property.

Innocent persons shall not suffer-no. But, if necessary, we will lead a wandering life, awaiting our opportunity to purge society of men so base that they degrade it with their opprobrium. As to land, Nature will always grant us sufficient to support our frames and we accept the consequences that may arise. Further, our personal enemies shall not possess our lands until they have fattened [them] with their own gore.

We cherish the hope, however, that the government, for the sake of its own dignity, and in obsequiousness to justice, will accede to our demand, by prosecuting those men and bringing them to trial, or leave them to become subject to the consequences of our immutable resolve.

Juan Nepomuceno Cortinas
Rancho Del Carmen
County of Cameron
September 30, 1859

Books

Anderson, Nancy, and Dwight Anderson. *The Generals: Ulysses S. Grant and Robert E. Lee*. New York: Alfred A. Knoff, 1988.

Arias, Juan de Dios. *Resena Historia de Ejercito del Norte durante la Invervencion Francesa*. Mexico: Impreta de Nabor Chavez, 1867.

Basch, Samuel. *Memories of Mexico: A History of the Last Ten Months of the Empire*, trans. by Hugh McAden Oechler. San Antonio: Trinity University Press, 1973.

Buenger, Walter L. *Secession and the Union in Texas*. Austin: University of Texas Press, 1984.

Cantu, Garcia Gaston. *El Socialismo en Mexico: Siglo XIX*. Mexico: Ediciones Era, 1969.

Del Castillo, Richard. *Treaty of Guadalupe Hidalgo: A Legacy of Conflict*. Oklahoma: University of Oklahoma Press, 1990.

-------. *The Los Angeles Barrio, 1850-1890: A Social History*. Berkeley: University of California Press, 1979.

De Leon, Arnoldo. *They Called Them Greasers: Anglo Attitudes Toward Mexicans in Texas, 1821-1900*. Austin: University of Texas Press, 1983.

Durham, George. *Taming the Nueces Strip: The Story of McNelly's Rangers*. Austin: University of Texas Press, 1962.

Flaquer, Mirabel Miro, ed. *Catalogo de Documentos- Carta de la Coleccion Porfirio Diaz-Tamaulipas, Marzo 1876-Noviembre 1885*. Ciudad Victoria: Universidad Autonoma de Tamaulipas, 1985.

Foote, Edward B. *Plain Home Talk Medical Common Sense*. New York: Murray Printing Co., 1858.

Hart, Mason John. *Anarchism & The Mexican Working Class, 1860-1931*. Austin: University of Texas Press, 1987.

Haslip, Joan. *The Crown of Mexico: Maximilian and His Empress Carlota*. New York: Holt, Rinehart and Winston, 1971.

Irby, James. *Backdoor at Bagdad: The Civil War on the Rio Grande.* El Paso: Texas Western Press, 1977.

Jennings, N.A. *A Texas Ranger.* New York: Charles Scribner's Sons, 1899.

Josephy, Alvin M. *The Civil War in the American West.* New York: Alfred A. Knopf, 1992.

Kearny, Milo, and Antony Knopp. *Boom and Bust: The Historical Cycles of Matamoros and Brownsville.* Austin: Eakin Press, 1991.

King, Edward, and J. Wells Champney. *Texas 1874, An Eyewitness Account of Conditions in Post-Reconstruction Texas, Robert S. Gray.* Houston: Cordovan Press, 1974.

Limon, Jose E. *Mexian Ballads, Chicano Poems: A History and Influence in Mexican-American Social Poetry.* Berkley: University of California Press, 1992.

McWhiney, Grady, and Sue McWhiney, eds. *To Mexico with Taylor and Scott, 1845-1847.* Waltham: Praisdell Publishing Co., 1969.

McWilliams, Carey. *North from Mexico: The Spanish Speaking People of the United States.* New York: Greenwood Press, 1968.

Meier, Matt S. *Mexican American Biographies: A Historical Dictionary, 1836-1987.* New York: Greenwood Press, 1988.

Montejano, David. *Anglos and Mexicanos in the Making of Texas, 1836-1986.* Austin: University of Texas Press, 1987.

Paredes, Americo. *Folklore and Culture on the Texas-Mexican Border.* Austin: University of Texas Press, 1993.

-------. *With his pistol in his hand.* Austin: University of Texas Press, 1958.

Schoonover, Thomas D. *Mexican Lobby: Matias Romero in Washington, 1861-1867.* Lexington: University Press of Kentucky, 1986.

Thompson, Jerry D. *Mexican Texans in the Union Army.* El Paso: University of Texas, 1986.

Webb, Walter Prescott. The Texas Rangers: A Century of Frontier Defense. Austin: University of Texas Press, 1965.
Williams, Hoyt John. *Sam Houston: A Biography of the Father of Texas.* New York: Simon and Schuster, 1993.

Newspapers

Brownsville *American Flag*
Brownsville *Herald*
Brownsville *Ranchero*
Corpus Christi *Ranchero*
Diario Oficial
El Zaragoza
Galveston *News*
Harper's Weekly
Los Angeles *Times*
New Orleans *Picayune*
New York *Times*
San Antonio *Express*
Voz del Pueblo

Oral History

Interviews conducted by Carlos Larralde.
Canales, Jose. Personal Interview. 10 May 1963; 6 April 1964; 10 April 1964; 15 April 1964; 9 June 1964; 10 June 1964; 12 June 1964; 24 June 1964; 27 June 1964; 28 June 1964; 10 July 1964; 12 August 1994; 15 August 1964; 12 November 1964; 16 November 1964; 18 November 1964; 24 August 1964; 30 August 1964.

Government Documents

United States. Reports of the Mexican Border Commission. Washington D.C., GPO, 1873.

------. U.S. War Department, The War of the Rebellion : A Compilation of the Official Records of the Union and Confederate Armies. Washington D.C., GPO, 1880-1901.

------. Cong. House. Committee on Military Affairs in Relation to the Texas Border Troubles. Testimony of Willian T. Sherman, 1877. 45th Congress. Con., 2nd sess., Serial No.1820. Washinton, D.C.: GPO, 1878.

------. The Conditions of Affairs in Mexico. by J. S. Ford to Tomas Mejia. 39th Cong., 1st. sess. H. Doc. 73. Washington D.C.: GPO, 1866.

------. Difficulties on the Southwestern Frontier. Affidavit of W.W. Nelson. 36th Cong., 1st sess. H. Doc. 52. Washington D.C.: Thomas H. Ford, Printer, 1860

Articles and Essays

Castellano, Antonio. "Por la Patria y Por la Raza" *Revista Mexico*, September 16, 1921.

Larralde, Carlos. "The Thoughts of Carlos Esparza," *Critica: A Journal of Critical Essays*, Vol.1 No.1, Spring 1984.

------. "J.T. Canales and the Texas Rangers," *The Journal of South Texas*, Vol.10, No.1, 1997.

------. "Juan Cortina's Spy: Elena Villareal de Ferrer," *The Journal of South Texas.*

McDonald, Russ. "Notorious Bandit," *Wild West*, October 1983, Nackman, Mark E. "Anglo-American Migrants to the West: Men of Broken Fortunes? The Case of Texas 1821-1846," *Western Historical Quarterly*, No.5 1974, p. 441-455.

Roebuck, Field. "Cheno Cortina: Red Robber of the Rio Grande," *True West*, September 1989.

A

Actos, 138, 141
Acuña, Rodolfo, 27, 34, 97,
    106, 114, 134, 140
Aguilas Damas, 121, 122
Aguilas Negras, 97, 106, 107,
    111, 149, 152
Alabanzas, 135, 140
American Civil War, 7, 51,
    54, 73, 78, 82, 83, 97,
    108, 121, 127, 131,
Anarchist, 47-49, 57
Anglos, 8,18, 19, 22, 24, 34,
    37, 39, 42, 44, 52, 54,
    65, 71, 108, 143, 145,
    146, 153
Arizona, 12, 16

B

Benavides, Santos, 82, 105,
    143
Blockade, 74-76, 81, 86, 154
Border (U. S./Mexico), 4-6,
    10, 16, 28, 31, 32, 34,
    35, 40, 44, 46, 50, 57-
    60, 64, 71, 72, 73, 74,
    76, 81, 82, 87-90, 95,
    106, 107, 109, 112,
    114,118, 120, 128, 131,
    133-136, 138, 140, 144,
    146, 153
Boston *Times*, 13

Brownsville, 5, 9, 10, 17, 26,
    29-32, 34-36, 43, 44, 46,
    50-53, 58-61, 64-69, 71,
    75, 78-81, 83, 89, 90,
    92, 93, 95, 97, 99, 102,
    113, 115, 123, 125, 128,
    131, 134, 136-140, 146,
    149, 152
Brownsville *Herald*, 5, 9, 26,
    34, 59-61, 71, 134, 138-
    140
Brownsville Rifles, 67
Brownsville Tigers, 66
Buchanan, James, 33

C

Cabrera, Tomas, 64
California, 3, 7, 12, 16, 19,
    22, 23, 27, 33, 37, 43,
    44, 56, 81, 83, 92, 101,
    138, 140, 141, 151, 154-
    156
Camargo, 4, 12, 22, 47
Cameron County (Texas), 31,
    37, 39, 43, 44, 57, 152
Canales, Jose T., 26, 29, 32,
    37, 38, 42, 43, 48-51,
    57, 82, 89, 98, 100,
    105, 123, 133, 134,
    144, 151
Chicano, 56, 120, 136-138,
    140, 141, 146

Juan N. Cortina

Chihuahua (Mexico), 33, 86
Colorado, 12, 16, 66, 81
Confederacy, 22, 51, 73-78,
    81, 82, 84, 90
Confederate soldiers, 7, 125
Corridos, 97, 135-138, 140,
    141
Cortinistas, 26, 29, 32, 33,
    38-41, 43, 46, 47-55
    57-59, 61, 64, 65,67-70,
    73, 75, 77-80, 82-86
    95, 99, 103-105, 107,
    112, 115, 119, 121, 123,
    131, 134-137, 143, 144,
    146, 149, 153, 154
Cotton, 4, 74-77, 82, 90, 99,
    146, 154
Curanderas, 42, 124-127

D
Defensores de la Patria, 38,
    98
Diaz, Porfirio, 9, 87, 88,
    119, 132, 140, 151, 156
Dupin, Charles, 84, 85, 151

E
Edwards, Haden, 11
El Hijo del Trabajo, 47-49
El Paso Salt War, 17
Esparza, Carlos, 8, 47, 48,
    57, 97, 104, 105, 109,
    117
Espiritu Santo Grant, 30, 35

Exploradores, 86-88, 98,
    101, 149, 152

F
Fieles, 82, 83, 85, 88, 95, 98,
    103, 106, 136, 149, 152
Flores, Carmen, 122
Ford, John S., 41, 90-92, 105
France, 16, 51, 70, 73, 75,
    77-87, 90-95, 97, 99,
    122, 123, 125, 131, 137
    150, 151, 154
French Intervention, 51, 73,
    83, 91

G
Garcia, Ramon, 105, 110
Germans, 19, 45, 50, 51, 99
Glaevecke, Adolphus, 31
Goldfinch, Charles, 64
Gold Rush, 3, 23
Gringos, 49, 50, 52, 71, 112
Grant, Ulysses S., 12, 14, 20,
    21
Griswold del Castillo, R., 17,
    22, 37, 44
Gutierrez, Jose Angel, 43,
    137

H
Haynes, John Leonard, 52
Heintzelman, Samuel P., 42,
    68